GIVE!

Who Gets Your Charity Dollar?

GIVE!

Who Gets Your Charity Dollar?

Harvey Katz

Anchor Press / Doubleday
Garden City, New York

1974

ISBN: 0-385-02220-4
Library of Congress Catalog Card Number 73–9163
Copyright © 1974 by Harvey Katz
All Rights Reserved
Printed in the United States of America
First Edition

To My Wife, Victoria

Author's Note

In the beginning, I was one of too many people who know much too little about American charity. After several months of research, I was indeed tempted to heed the advice of a charity executive: "You've bitten off more than you can chew, young man. If I were you, I'd forget about this and try something simpler. You'll never finish this book." That I kept going is attributable in large part to the encouragement and assistance of two friends and business associates: David Obst, my agent, and Bill Whitehead, my editor. I am very grateful.

Many people provided me with vital information after I agreed not to identify them as sources of information. The book could not have been written without their help. I am also indebted to several writers who addressed various aspects of American charity long before I began my research. I found two books particularly helpful: *The Gentle Legions,* by Richard Carter (Doubleday, 1961), and *Fund Raising in the United States,* by Scott Cutlip (Rutgers, 1965).

Contents

Introduction

On this day, you and I and our fellow American contributors donated over $55 million and countless hours of volunteer talent to charitable organizations across the nation. We made a similar investment yesterday and we will do the same tomorrow. We are indeed generous people.

American charity has given us much in return. There are such tangible benefits as a national blood supply, disaster-relief services, cures for several diseases, and assistance to the disabled, the disenfranchised, and the needy. By their very existence, charities offer us meaningful ways to devote a part of our lives to a selfless purpose. Without American charity, our society would be much less pleasant and our lives far less human.

We would not commit over $20 billion each year to philanthropy if we were not aware of these things. At the same time, there is a great deal we do not know about our charities. We don't actually see the food that feeds the hungry child in India or the research scientist whose salary we are paying. And while we know what we are giving up to fulfill our end of the relationship, we have no way of estimating what charity is giving in return. How much should a cure for polio cost? What is a child's smile worth? These are priceless commodities, of course, and we have no right to expect a price tag. But we do indeed have a right to expect our charities to make the best possible use of our donations. We hope they do. But we are not absolutely certain.

There are two options: We can continue on the same path, shrugging off our doubts and hoping for the best. Or we can seek out the obvious antidote: information on how American charity works and on whether it works well. This book is founded on the premise that the second path, while the more difficult one, is better for everyone and everything involved in the charity relationship—contributors, recipients, volunteers, charitable organizations, faith, compassion, and charity itself.

The book is written for the benefit of the average American contributor. This viewpoint was adopted for several reasons. Among them is the obvious fact that it is our money that fuels the charity system. If anyone has a right to know, we do. Equally important, among all the interests that are vested in American charity, the contributor's is the only one that is completely selfless. If the system isn't working for the benevolently inspired, it is not working as it should. That is what charity is about.

This seems to be a unique approach to charity, and it dictates certain departures from traditional thinking. There are, for example, several types of enterprises that are not usually considered charitable but which nevertheless actually compete for a share of the charitable dollar. These include the lobby groups, patriotic organizations, and similar enterprises that solicit financial support from the general public by holding out a worthy cause and appealing to our charitable instincts. Whatever their titles or tax statuses, such organizations cannot be ignored in any contributor-oriented study of the charity business. At the same time, there are eleemosynary institutions such as colleges, churches, and hospitals that do not reach out to the average contributor, but, rather, appeal to select groups of people who have a special involvement with the institution itself. These enterprises fall outside the scope of this book.

It would be ludicrous to commence an investigation by insulating the subject of inquiry from possible reproach. It thus becomes necessary to set aside the reverence that customarily attaches to organizations that operate in the name of charity. Undoubtedly, some people will take offense at the unawed language that follows and conclude that it indicates anti-benevolent feelings on the part of the author. Quite the contrary is true.

Part 1

The Charity World

1   A Noble Crusade

American charity is founded on the many sacrifices of some very courageous people. Clara Barton, for example, was a remarkable person who became this nation's legendary "angel of mercy" during a lifetime of selfless service. She set up soup kitchens on a score of Civil War battlefields. She tended the sick and wounded as shells burst around her. She drove her wagon, alone and unprotected, through the fiercest fighting of the war. It was a time when wounded were left to rot by the thousands where they fell, when minor wounds and simple illnesses would result in death for lack of care. Barton saw it all.

So when the war ended, she set out to establish a civilian hospital corps for this nation's armed forces. In many ways, it was her toughest battle. She encountered both the peacetime apathy of the American public and the outright disdain of the social elite toward what they considered bleeding-heart do-goodery. People should take care of themselves; right? Anyone who needs help must be a lazy beggar; right? These were the attitudes that Barton fought.

Clara Barton was only one of several noble Americans who became charity pioneers around the turn of the century: Jane Addams went into the Chicago slums to establish Hull House and demonstrate that, contrary to what the elite were saying, poor children could rise above their environment and become self-sufficient and productive, given the necessary help and encouragement. Lillian Wald did much the same with the Henry Street Settlement, in New York City. My father is a Henry Street alumnus. He and others who catapulted out of the slums remember the settlement house as one of the very few bright spots in what was probably the worst ghetto in America.

The need for the charity pioneers was critical. Wave after wave of immigrants descended on the land of dreams to find only slums and sweatshops. Tuberculosis was a deadly killer that could spread like wildfire, claiming three times as many lives as did cancer, while the medical profession continued to insist that TB was not a contagious disease. Dr. Lawrence Flick, who fathered the voluntary health movement by establishing the Pennsylvania Society for the Prevention of Tuberculosis, was ridiculed by doctors and denounced as a charlatan for contending that tuberculosis was indeed contagious and fostered by filthy TB wards and unsanitary living conditions.

It was as though the physicians and the rest of the establishment did not want to know the truth, perhaps out of fear of realizing that tuberculosis and other plagues of the time were caused, not by fate or ethnic background or laziness, but by a society that made victims of its citizens, a society that covered the slummy side of life with a smile and pretended it did not exist. The charity pioneers were frustrated time and again. But they kept coming. The personal compassion and outrage of the Flicks and the Bartons became a viable social force, a people's movement for a better life.

The flames were fed by writers such as Upton Sinclair, who dramatized the horrors of American working life. The need was compounded by World War I, burdening the nation with war casualties in staggering numbers. But, for the most part, the establishment continued to resist. Clara Barton won a Congressional charter for the Red Cross in 1900, but this was almost entirely a personal triumph rather than one for American charity. The nation did indeed respond with considerable generosity to Red Cross war drives nearly two decades later, but this was clearly an act of patriotism, not of charity. The struggle continued. The poor and the sick were still regarded as beggars.

The breakthrough came under the impact of three events that had a profound impact on just about every phase of American life. First came the Depression, the great leveler. Corporate executives who only weeks before had been disdaining those in need of charity were now in desperate need themselves—in need of assistance that did not exist, because of the same corporate executives and their golf partners in government. Their resistance to the concept of charity would never be quite as adamant again. But the Depression alone probably would not have been enough. Money has a way of shortening memories.

The second event was the election of Franklin D. Roosevelt to the presidency. Whether by reason of his own moral code or the demand of national necessity, Roosevelt initiated some dramatic new views on social responsibility for Americans, and with his extraordinary personal appeal he was able to make a rather large dent in nineteenth-century disdain for charity. Roosevelt's election also gave the nation a polio-stricken President. This alone probably would have been sufficient to launch the massive anti-polio campaign that ushered in a new era for American charity. In fact, Basil O'Connor, who masterminded the polio drive, was a long-time friend of Roosevelt, and he entered the charity field at the President's request.

Finally came America's entry into the Second World War. While the war in the Pacific appears to have been thrust upon us, this did not seem to be the case in Europe. From outward appearances at least, we were there because we wanted to be there. We were knights in shining armor. We would appear from a distant land, rescue the enslaved peoples, and then ride off into the sunset. It was a wonderful self-image. And it automatically discredited nearly all opposition to the concept of American charity. Good knights do not weigh the culpability of the maiden in distress. If she is being victimized at the time, there is an obligation to rescue her. So it was with America. We sacrificed life to aid the victims of tyranny. How could we refuse to sacrifice mere time and money in order to aid victims of war, poverty, and disease? We could not. And the early 1940s saw a raft of new charitable organizations arise in America, and others that had theretofore been struggling for existence found new public acceptance during their fund-raising campaigns. And now, rather than oppose our charitable enterprises, the social elite did an abrupt about-face and clamored for control of them. For the most part, they were successful.

Today, American charity is very much like America itself—born of a heroic rebellion against an insensitive establishment, but now an established institution itself—
wealthy, powerful, and respectable. A great many of our
charity board members come from the corporate world. They
are supplemented by people from the top rungs of the legal
and medical professions and by women who appear regularly on the society pages.

A new social elite has arisen in America since Clara Barton's day. It is very much in evidence among our charities.
In 1971, for example, the national chairman of the National
Easter Seal Society was none other than America's favorite
doctor, Marcus Welby, portrayed on television by actor
Robert Young. In 1972, the national chairman of the Epilepsy Foundation of America was movie actor Jack Lemmon. And it is becoming increasingly difficult to turn on a
television set without encountering Bob Hope, Zsa Zsa Gabor, George Jessel, Billy Graham, or a celebrity of equal
fame, appealing for donations to some worthy cause. They
join in a massive celebrity parade, providing American
charity with a prestige and a glamour unequaled by any
other American institution.

Sometimes, there is more than glitter. Every September,
for example, Jerry Lewis devotes twenty-four sleepless hours
on television to the Muscular Dystrophy Associations of
America. You can't watch him for very long without realizing that he cares very much about the afflicted children
he is trying to help. Even if you wouldn't pay a dime to see
one of his movies, you find it very difficult indeed to resist
his obvious sincerity and compassion. You want to join him,
to help make those children healthy and happy. And the
longer you watch, the closer you feel to what is happening
on the other side of your television screen.

The studio is crammed with people well into the wee

hours. Local television stations break in periodically to show their own celebrities out on street corners, flagging down motorists to ask for contributions. The amount of pledged donations is revealed on a large electric signboard. As the figure approaches a round number, the audience pitches in with dimes and dollars. All of us wait with growing excitement until the signboard changes to a long row of zeroes. And then, even at home, we cheer triumphantly. We have reached our goal.

It is a crusade in the classic sense: a charismatic leader, a worthy cause, a band of devoted followers. There is a bit of hokum involved, of course, but hokum has become part of nearly every phase of American life. It is a riskless type of crusading compared to the ventures of King Richard I. But its purpose is certainly far more noble than Richard's search for blood and glory. And a charity crusade is not without some sacrifice. Jerry Lewis and his associates could have found easier ways to conduct a charity campaign. And they certainly could have devoted those telethon hours to a less demanding and more selfish purpose. By their grace, we are put in touch with charity, at least for a moment. We are given a chance to share the dreams and compassion and excitement of good people, people who care.

The crusading spirit is very much in evidence elsewhere in the charity world, particularly during campaigns run by the United Way of America. In many of our cities, enormous United Way signs are stretched across downtown thoroughfares. There is an incredible media blitz, fashioned by volunteer talent from the best ad agencies on Madison Avenue. In government agencies and in factories and other business enterprises, campaign people ask their fellow employees to join the crusade by donating part of their salaries to United Way charities. It is done mostly on volunteer talent. Everyone pitches in. And in 1971, everyone pitched in to the tune of $800 million. It sounds like a staggering amount. But Americans donated over $20 billion to philanthropy that year. Even if we eliminate the religious and educational institutions that appeal to select groups of people, it means that United Way has been attracting less than 10 per cent of the American charity dollar. Something is missing, of course. The words sound right and the techniques should be effective. United Way has goodness, glamour, talent, and tradition. But United Way does not have Margaret.

Margaret is a little girl with beautiful eyes who lives in Calcutta, India. I received her photograph the other day, compliments of the Christian Children's Fund, together with a brochure that tells me Margaret is dying of malnutrition and her life can be saved for twelve dollars a month. I have looked into that little girl's eyes for a very long time, and feeding Margaret has become a lot more important to me than celebrities, slogans, and pretty music. Margaret is the heart of American charity—the someone or something to make better. And United Way of America—a vast conglomerate of charities we do not know—does not really have a Margaret it can hold up to us. It crusades in the name of charity alone, and that is not quite enough. Crusading is an inspirational business. In order to participate fully, we need a clear, identifiable cause to move us. Realizing this, many charitable organizations have refused to merge their various causes with those of United Way members. And some of them have done very nicely indeed.

There is no shortage of causes in the charity world. If you sit down and invent a cause that sounds worthy, chances are good that there is an organization already in existence that appeals to the American public in the name of that cause. The dictionary tells us that charity means giving alms to the poor. But that definition was devised long before diseases became conquerable; before social betterment could be wrought through court suits, picketing, and grass-roots lobbying. From our viewpoint as contributors, dictionary definitions and Internal Revenue rulings are meaningless. We allocate a certain part of our earnings and perhaps our time for worthy causes. An organization that asks us for some of that time and money is a charity for our purposes— no matter what banner it flies, regardless of its shape or size. The list includes civil-rights groups as well as health charities. There are countless organizations dedicated to feeding hungry people, both here and abroad. Others devote their time and money to helping the handicapped, conservation, mental health, birth control, culture, political action. Just leaf through their names: Korean Relief, Free Europe, Freedom from Hunger, CARE. They do indeed seem to form a vast crusade for a better world and a better life.

Spearheaded by these noble causes, canonized by the sacrifices of Barton and the rest, glamorized by the celebrities, packaged by Madison Avenue, and blessed by the President of the United States, Bob Hope, and Billy Graham, American charity reaches out and asks for our support. It fills our mailboxes, glitters across our television screens, and sings through our radios. It appeals to the best side of us. And we do indeed respond. Despite our numerous shortcomings, we are good people, compassionate people, crusading people. We want to end suffering, cure disease, and raise up the disenfranchised. We have been generous to the organizations that say they share these goals with us, generous with both our money and our faith. Perhaps too generous.

2   A Secret Organization

CHARITY ASKS FOR DONATIONS! CITES AFFLICTED CHILDREN!
—Washington, D.C. The United Cerebral Palsy Associations issued a nationwide appeal today for money. Referring
to "a lot of children" afflicted with the disease, the Cerebral
Palsy group stated that the best way to help "those children
lead normal lives" is to make out a check immediately.
Former television great Shari Lewis issued the following
public statement: "Please, PLEASE, give all you can. You
can help this girl WALK to her Daddy. So, please, please,
please, PLEASE be generous." Dennis James, the famed

promoter of the dancing cigarette package, endorsed the campaign, stating: "If Moe's Sporting Goods can give $100, you can certainly spare something." James indicated that the group would accept anything from "a dime to a dollar." Ms. Lewis candidly added: "Please, please give from the heart. Please give all you can. Please do your part. PLEASE!"

It actually happened on January 28, 1973, when Shari Lewis, Dennis James, *et al.* titillated our television sets with a semiextravaganza imaginatively entitled "Celebrity Parade for Cerebral Palsy." I learned quite a bit from several hours of viewing. I learned that Shari Lewis has a favorite word and that she is breathless. Someone named Smiley, or maybe it was Jack, told me: "We got Moe's Sporting Goods for a hundred dollars. We got Harry's Liquor Store for fifty dollars." And so on. I learned that I could join in all the fun, help one of the beautiful children that the TV camera found so irresistible, and boost the numbers on the big signboard, just by picking up my telephone and pledging a contribution. But there was one thing I did not learn: exactly what would be done with the money I was forking over. I was told nothing about fund-raising costs or administrative expenses. Nothing about how much Cerebral Palsy actually spends to help the children whom it uses to attract my donation.

So I decided to resist Ms. Lewis' impassioned plea for an immediate contribution and first find out how my money would be spent. I wrote to Cerebral Palsy national headquarters and asked for a copy of its annual report. In due course, I received a slickly produced brochure that contains photographs of scientists, celebrities, and, of course, beautiful children. I read through pages and pages of promotional material, a list of research grants, and finally I came to the Cerebral Palsy financial statement. Yes! An honest-to-

goodness, unglamorized statement of where my money
would go. But then I noticed that the financial statement has
a "Note 1" that says these figures apply only to national
headquarters, which receives only a "designated portion" of
contributions. And after searching every corner of the annual report, I still did not know the amount of that "designated portion" or the amount of total contributions and
expenses. I still did not know how much of the Cerebral
Palsy charitable dollar is devoted to a charitable purpose.

I looked in the telephone directory and learned that the
Washington Cerebral Palsy affiliate is located at 1028 Connecticut Avenue. This turned out to be a high-rise office
building. The Cerebral Palsy door turned out to be closed
and locked. No one answered my several minutes of loud
knocking.

I telephoned the United Givers Fund (UGF), Washington's United Way organization, and was told that, yes, at
least one Cerebral Palsy affiliate in the area gets UGF
funds and, yes, if I came down to the UGF building I
could look at the Cerebral Palsy financial statement. But
when I arrived at the UGF five minutes later, I was treated
like an alien invader, shuttled from one office to another,
and finally told that UGF has nothing to do with financial
data. That is the responsibility of the Health & Welfare
Council (HWC), the UGF affiliate that decides how UGF
funds are distributed.

I then went downstairs to the HWC offices and, after still
more shuttling, I found myself with Thomas Fetzer, Deputy
Director of the HWC. "Why, yes," Fetzer told me, "we have
that kind of information. But I can't let you see it. Those
reports are confidential. Besides, they would only mislead
you. Take this instead." He handed me a report the size
of a telephone book. "You'll find everything you want to
know in there," Fetzer said. "In fact, we've been accused

of overreporting. We think it's our responsibility here to keep the public fully informed."

The volume Fetzer gave me is the 1972 report of the HWC Membership and Budget Committee. It is an incredible document. For each of the eighty-plus charities in the Washington area that receives UGF funds, there is a lengthy discussion of the organization's objectives, the number of blacks on its staff, the number of blacks that should be on its staff, and why there aren't more blacks on its staff. In almost every case, there is a commendation for some good project the charity has undertaken. Now and then there is a recommendation to "consolidate some services" or "achieve maximum utilization of resources." Included are color-coordinated indexes, cross indexes, lists of rules and regulations, and committee memberships. It adds up to over three pounds of paper on my scales. But there is not one ounce in there on administrative fund-raising or program costs, not one word to tell us how those UGF charities have been spending our contributions.

Until recently, Howard Kresge was executive director of the State Department's Advisory Committee on Voluntary Foreign Aid.[1] As such, he maintained financial data on more than eighty charities that assist people overseas. "I'd like to help you," Kresge told me. "But those reports are confidential. They would mislead you anyway." Kresge did not have a telephone book to give me. Instead, he suggested that I write to his eighty-plus charities individually and ask for copies of their annual reports. I did. About forty per cent of the organizations I contacted did not honor me with a reply. Half of those that did reply failed to send me any financial data whatsoever—just a glossy brochure and an envelope large enough for my check.

So I telephoned the Internal Revenue Service (IRS) and

[1] Kresge retired from government service shortly before publication.

was told that all tax-exempt organizations are required to file annual informational returns with the IRS and that these returns are public information. If I would come down to the IRS offices, fill out an application for each organization, wait a few weeks, and come back to the IRS offices, I would get the information I wanted, without evasion or sudden substitution. But I soon learned that the odds are very much in favor of encountering even more frustration at the IRS. For one thing, American charities do not exactly rush to the IRS with their informational returns. In late 1972 I requested information on a long list of organizations. According to the IRS, none of these had yet filed their 1971 returns. Many had not even filed their returns for 1970. Equally important, a significant number of returns that are filed turn out to be masterpieces of non-information. Not surprisingly, the amount of information a charity discloses to the IRS seems directly related to the efficiency of the charitable organization and the political clout of its supporters.

The Freedoms Foundation at Valley Forge, founded by the late Dwight D. Eisenhower, did not file its 1969 informational return until February 1972. On that return, the Foundation stated that it had raised $1 million at a cost of 45 per cent of receipts. In explaining its $543,780 in "Miscellaneous Expenses," the Foundation listed, among other things, $112,000 for "Professional Services," $105,000 in "Travel Expenses," and $110,000 in more "Miscellaneous Expenses," which the organization did not bother to itemize. The major activity of this charity seems to be issuing hundreds of cash awards, prizes, and medals to individuals who contribute to "strengthening the American Credo."

A revealing insight into what the Freedoms Foundation views as the "American Credo" is provided by my previous book, *Shadow on the Alamo* (Doubleday, 1972), which discusses how two recent Freedoms Foundation award winners, Jack Cox and Will Wilson, were knee-deep in the quick-buck schemes of Frank Sharp, the Houston promoter who bribed several Texas state officials and defrauded his own bank depositors of $20 million. Wilson allowed Sharp to use his bank account as a conduit for at least one "loan" to a federal bank examiner. Cox was an officer of several business entities that Sharp used to work his way to financial stardom.

The champion of the non-information return is undoubtedly the prestigious, though recently controversial, United States Olympic Committee. In 1968, that organization explained nearly $900,000 in "Miscellaneous Expenses" with such illuminating items as "Promotional Expenses" ($396,000), "Administrative Expenses" ($222,000), and "Olympic Trials" ($265,000). In 1969, it spent over 50 per cent of its receipts on promotion and fund raising, and nearly all the rest on general administration.

A few state legislatures have passed progressive charity-disclosure laws. But if a charitable institution wishes to remain secretive about its finances, it can simply avoid soliciting in those states. Better yet, an organization with sufficient political clout (and there are a lot of charities with sufficient political clout) can use its influence to obtain a statutory exemption for itself. The state of Wisconsin has a far-reaching charity-disclosure law that has one peculiar exemption: a Congressionally chartered veterans' organization does not have to disclose anything to anyone. Now, it so happens that the biggest Congressionally chartered veterans' organization soliciting funds on a mass-appeal basis is the Disabled American Veterans, which happens to be one of the last charities that should be exempted from anything (see chapter 8).

What goes on here? By any standard, charities are public

enterprises. They are endorsed by public idols, given free time and space by public media, granted extraordinary licenses by public agencies, and, of course, they are succored by contributions from the general public. As such, they should certainly be open to public scrutiny. They are not. To be sure, many charities are forthright about their activities. But, at the same time, a conspiracy of silence runs through much of the charity world. You see it in the vagaries of annual reports and informational tax returns. You encounter it on the sealed lips of people such as Thomas Fetzer and Howard Kresge. And even while speaking to representatives of the most worthwhile charities, you find the same reflexive tendency to deny, defend, and forgive shenanigans considered outrageous in the business world. In a candid moment, they might tell you, yes, it's a terrible thing, but we're all in the same boat here. If one charity gets a black eye, all charities suffer. If it's done in the name of charity, then, the public must not know. The skeletons must remain in their tax-deductible closets.

American charity asks for our money by holding up a glittering mask of noble causes, celebrity endorsements, biblical myths, and Madison Avenue imagery. In the iciness of our minds, we know it is mostly nonsense. But how often do we think about it? Perhaps a few moments each year. During those few moments, American charity tells us to "give from the heart," not the brain. It asks us to swallow it all whole, hoping that we will be moved by love, hate, fear, idol worship, or some other blinding emotion to abandon our common sense and rush to the checkbook.

In this respect, American charity is no different from the auto repairman who lures you into his shop with promises of a free tune-up and then sells you a transmission you don't need. The Federal Trade Commission had just initiated action against several carpet stores in the Washington area for advertizing three rooms of carpeting and really selling only one room and two closets of carpeting. Is it any less deceptive to advertise charity in such glowing terms without warning the contributor that his dollar can be short-circuited to pay for fund raising, promotion, and similar expenses?

No matter how noble the cause that is dangled before our eyes, the money we donate goes to an organization, not to the cause itself. And that organization can be crooked, misguided, inept, wasteful, and vulnerable to a million other failings that will divert the charity dollar from its intended purpose. This is the deepest secret of the charity world. Not that fund-raising costs are high, but that fund-raising costs are incurred at all. Not that a charitable organization can be shoddily managed, but that the organization exists at all. They would rather we believe that in the heavenly charity world our donation is magically transmitted from our hand directly to the crippled child or research scientist.

There are some obvious advantages. For one thing, those strong emotional appeals would lose considerable impact if our minds were filled with questions about the organization handling our money. No longer would a critic of the Disabled American Veterans be attacked as an enemy of the disabled and a disbeliever in charity itself. No longer would the American contributor assume that the charity must be perfect because it is a charity, because the President of the United States endorses it, or because it stands for the things that made this country great. Rather, our charitable organizations would be forced to appeal to us as intelligent human beings and ask for our support on the basis of their accomplishments. Ironically, most of our charities could, in fact, win our support on that basis. They could trot out their financial statements during tomorrow's telethons, lay it on the line, and win a standing ovation. But they won't do it, apparently for two reasons. First, it would take time and money to explain their expenditures adequately. Second, that glittering façade is so contrary to reality that they fear we will turn away from charity altogether when we learn the truth. Better to deceive us and thrive than to risk our outrage.

The charity façade, however, cannot stand forever. We are starting to wise up, after having been kicked around all these years. Someday, we will take a good look at Zsa Zsa Gabor during her next telethon appearance. We will remember that she is the same Zsa Zsa Gabor who, in a TV commercial, pushed AAMCO, the transmission company that, according to the FTC, happily ripped off the American consumer to the tune of untold millions. Or we will start thinking about Margaret, dying of malnutrition in that Calcutta alleyway, and we will wonder what happened after the Christian Children's Fund snapped her photograph. Was Margaret left in the alleyway to die, or is the Christian Children's Fund just putting us on?

The dark side of the charity world is becoming headline material. Recently, few newspaper readers could avoid learning the incredible tale of Father Flanagan's Boys Town, of movie fame, and how it has amassed more millions than it could use in a decade while continuing to wave pictures of raggedy orphans before our eyes. Racial discrimination by United Way has been getting top billing on the editorial page, while the good work of the dedicated volunteer is fortunate to win an inch in the features section.

So long as American charity continues its secret ways, we can expect an already bruised American consumer to become increasingly disenchanted. We read that the Thomas A. Dooley Foundation has just given Frank Sinatra some kind of most-charitable-person award, just two months after Sinatra uncharitably shouted drunken obscenities at a reporter in a Washington restaurant. What are we supposed to believe? What will American charity offer us to counteract the impression that it has been losing sight of itself, that it is wallowing in empty-headed celebrities, meaningless slogans, and political apple-polishing? Another telethon? Another heartbeat?

Well, it just won't do. They are fiddling around with a lot more than our money. We're vulnerable enough as consumers. But, in the marketplace, we are at least dealing with something tangible most of the time. Not so in the charity world—we can't kick the tires of the Red Cross before sending in a donation. We are at the mercy of our own faith. And in these times, faith is much too valuable a commodity to be taken lightly. We have been too often victimized because we believed a promise, trusted another human being, or relied on our own hope.

Can we, in fact, help each other? Are we capable of dealing intelligently with the truth? Are we really selfless people, or mere idol worshipers? American charity refuses to put us to the test. We are left with three choices: we can wash our hands of the whole business, we can grope along in blind support and hope that the roof doesn't fall in someday, or we can try to find out the truth—for Margaret's sake as well as our own.

Part 2

The Charity Business

3 Profiteering: The Grand Illusion

If there be among you a needy man, one of thy brethren, within any of thy gates, in thy land which the Lord thy God giveth thee, thou shalt not harden thy heart, nor shut thy hand from thy needy brother; but thou shalt surely open thy hand unto him, and shalt surely lend him sufficient for his need in that which he wanteth. . . . Thou shalt surely give him, and thy heart shall not be grieved for when thou givest unto him. Deuteronomy 15:7–10.

In a truly primitive society, setting up an effective charity system requires solving two problems. First, it is necessary to overcome instinctive human selfishness in order to insure that people who have excess food and shelter will make such things available to the needy. Equally important is the manner in which they are made available. If charity is doled out with disdain and ridicule, some very needy people may well choose suffering instead. So we set out rules and teachings to deal with these two problems and leave it at that. Our charity system is far from perfect. But it's the best we can do under the circumstances.

Unfortunately, time moves a lot faster than do our rules and teachings. And, incredible as it may seem, many of the ideas that grew out of that primitive charity system are very much alive today, regardless of their validity. For example, plenty of people continue to believe that the only problems facing our billion-dollar charity institution are overcoming the selfishness of the wealthy and making sure that the needy will not be too embarrassed to ask for help. If we can just accomplish these two things, they believe, everything will run smoothly. Another biblical carryover is the idea that profit is the direct antithesis of charity. Here again, the idea was perfectly reasonable in that primitive civilization. There was absolutely no way you could benefit, in a material sense, from leaving a corner of your field to the poor. It was a simple accounting transaction and the contributor inevitably wound up on the debit side. And yet, even in later biblical years, a changing world had already dated the principle.

Woe unto them that decree unrighteous decrees, And to the writers that write iniquity; To turn aside the needy from judgment, And to take away the right of the poor of My people, That widows may be their spoil, And that they may make the fatherless their prey! Isaiah, 10:1–2.

Charity had become more organized by that time, more civilized. And a natural consequence of both organization and civilization is corruption. Middlemen were introduced into the charity system, to levy tithes, to collect and dole out charity to the needy. If there is one principle that applies to all civilizations, it is that middlemen will somehow manage to make a profit from any enterprise, no matter how non-profit and beneficent it might appear. So it was that in Isaiah's day, the collectors, keepers, and distributors of charitable contributions made widows their spoil and the fatherless their prey. And so it has been ever since.

During the mid-1950s, Washington attorney Victor Orsinger became the financial adviser to a Catholic religious order and charity, the Society of the Divine Saviour. Orsinger presented himself to the Society as a financial wizard and wealthy philanthropist who would dramatically increase the organization's charitable capital. Appearances supported these grand claims. At the time, Orsinger was living on the 5,000-acre Chrysler estate near Warrenton, Virginia. He had a private plane and a helicopter at his disposal, and he used both to ferry celebrities to his lavish parties.

What was not so apparent, and what the Society of the Divine Saviour did not bother to determine, was that Victor Orsinger's real estate empire was operating on a razor-thin margin and that it desperately needed liquid assets to survive, and that no matter how benevolent Orsinger appeared, he was really very much out for himself. What he wanted was not only the Society's considerable wealth, but its good name as well.

The first step of every successful white-collar criminal is to erect a respectable façade behind which to operate, a façade that will hide the questionable dealings and, at the same time, allay the suspicions of prospective victims. There can be no better organization for this purpose than a charity, the mythically perfect entity that no one dares question and everyone blindly favors. And so it was. Not only did Orsinger appropriate several hundred thousand dollars in Society assets for his own use, he also used the organization as a front for numerous dubious business schemes. In several cases, his victims suspected they were being taken, but they hesitated to go to court, because Orsinger was dealing through the Society. "We should have filed suit against all of them immediately," the head of an investment group victimized by Orsinger told me. "But our lawyers said it would probably come down to our word against the word of a Catholic charity and that half the judges in Washington are Catholic."

In order to gain the confidence of the priests who were running the Society of the Divine Saviour, Victor Orsinger capitalized on the ancient myth that charity and profit never mix. He gave huge sums to Catholic causes, even while he was stealing other Catholic groups blind. A tract of land he donated to Washington's Patrick Cardinal O'Boyle had, in fact, been saved from foreclosure with money Orsinger embezzled from the Sisters of the Divine Saviour in Milwaukee, a charity he defrauded out of more than a million dollars.

Texas promoter Frank Sharp victimized another Catholic charity, the Jesuit Fathers of Houston, in almost identical fashion. Sharp won the confidence of this organization by giving it a large tract of land and appointing its top executive, Father Michael Kennelly, as a director of Sharp's bank. Apparently, Kennelly was the first priest bank director in history. He was so moved by the honor that he gave Frank Sharp $6 million in charitable funds, which Sharp never repaid. Kennelly also served as a middleman in Sharp's bribery of the Speaker of the Texas House of Representatives and several other high state officials.

The Jesuit Fathers arranged a most extraordinary honor for a man who was knee-deep in charity fraud, embezzlement, and bribery. As Father Kennelly testified during a Securities and Exchange Commission (SEC) deposition: "He was honored by the Father General of the Jesuit Order, and, upon our recommendation in Houston to our principal superior, and after due consultation, and that this honor involved being a founder of the New Orleans Province of the Society of Jesus, that he was the first Protestant since the Order was founded to obtain this honor, he and his family, and that in obtaining it certain documents and so forth, banquets were held in Rome, and he was given an audience, his entire family, with his children and their husbands, with the Holy Father, and the Holy Father made a great deal of it and gave a little speech on the occasion." So it was that the Pope gave his blessings to Frank Sharp. And in 1971, after the SEC and the national press revealed what Sharp had really been up to, the Pope sent a telegram expressing his sympathy and advising Sharp that prayers were being said in Rome on his behalf. All for a tract of land and a bank directorship!

Frank Sharp, Victor Orsinger, and the priests and nuns who, wittingly or not, helped them defraud innocent contributors did not benefit in the long run from their dealings. Sharp's financial empire crumbled and he barely escaped criminal punishment by doing a deal with then Deputy Attorney General Richard Kleindienst. Orsinger was convicted of larceny and, as of this writing, is serving a jail sentence. All the Catholic organizations involved with these two men went bankrupt. And yet there were indeed some substantial immediate profits made in these transactions by people who had successfully palmed themselves off as great benefactors and representatives of charitable organizations.

Frank Sharp and Victor Orsinger were only part-time charity profiteers. During the course of other business ventures, they simply picked up the Catholic groups, exploited them for what they were worth, and then continued on their way. Equally prominent in the charity business is the outright promoter, the person who builds an entire business enterprise on charity-for-profit. Such a business person does not waste time seeking out naïve middlemen like Father Kennelly to exploit. After all, the American contributor is equally vulnerable, equally blinded by the charity myths, and, in many respects, even more exploitable.

Patrick J. Gorman is a Washington fund raiser. He specializes in politically conservative groups that appeal to middle America in the name of Spiro Agnew, the FBI, and even the Bible itself. Gorman bears little resemblance to the usual professional fund-raising consultant, whose job it is to assist charitable organizations in developing sound fund-raising techniques, obtaining government grants, and such. For one thing, Gorman is often directly involved in creating and managing the groups he represents—a practice that is off limits for the true fund-raising consultant. More important, Gorman's past activities strongly indicate that he is much less interested in helping the groups he represents than in serving Patrick Gorman. His usual method of operation is to find a paper organization already in existence, in most cases formed by well-meaning people who did not have the time or money to get their charitable project off the ground. The existing organization holds two attractions for Gorman: first, a façade behind which to do business without showing himself; second, a tax exemption from the IRS. Gorman meets with the people who formed the paper organization and either deludes them completely as to what he has in mind or lures them into the rewarding game of charity profiteering. Gorman's next step is to create a second entity with a name more suitable for conservative fund raising, bring this entity under the umbrella of the first, and then launch a massive direct-mail campaign with mailing lists he has perfected through years and years of similar enterprises. If possible, Gorman obtains the endorsement of a well-known conservative celebrity to help attract donations.

Take the United Police Fund, for example. This Gorman enterprise was launched in 1970 for the ostensible purpose of helping widows of slain policemen. Before getting underway, Gorman obtained the co-operation of three people who had previously formed the Public Trust Foundation, a Washington group that had accomplished nothing except obtaining one of those tax exemptions. The Public Trust people say they were completely deceived by Patrick Gorman (and there is no reason to disbelieve them). Gorman wrote a fund-raising brochure and letter and somehow induced Congressman Sam Devine (R., Ohio) to sign the letter. Devine now says he was also deceived. The brochure contains photographs of policemen standing around a grave. It talks about law-and-order and certain kinds of Americans wanting to ruin our nation.

The United Police Fund raised $110,000 in two years. Of this amount, $80,000 was paid to Patrick Gorman. The Public Trust Foundation people say that this only partly paid Gorman's fees and expenses. He asked for a lot more, but they have refused to pay it. They divided what was left between widows of slain policemen and the executive director of the United Police Fund. The Public Trust people say they have fired Gorman and hope to continue without him. But they note that the number of future beneficiaries has been somewhat reduced by the fact that the police departments of New York City and Los Angeles County have barred their employees from any involvement whatsoever with the United Police Fund.

Gorman's usual retainer is $2,500 monthly. He also receives reimbursement for any out-of-pocket expenses, to which he adds an additional 18 per cent. This markup is justified by Gorman on the ground that he obtains printing and materials at lower rates than anyone else and he himself should get the benefit of these savings. In addition to the retainer and the markup, Gorman also charges his "clients" for the use of his mailing lists. So, all in all, it is a pretty good way to make a living.

Gorman's most profitable single enterprise was probably "Friends of the FBI." Everyone who was involved in this non-charity campaign is now scurrying to deny involvement or claim innocence. So it is pretty difficult to paint a complete picture. But, from all indications, the idea seems to have been conceived by Lee Edwards, a Washington public-relations consultant, lover of conservative causes, and friend of Patrick Gorman. The idea was simple: defend the image of the FBI, which at the time was being tarnished by the despicable longhairs and the biased media. More accurately, raise money for the cause of defending the FBI image. For their paper organization Gorman and Edwards chose the Commission for International Due Process of Law, in Chicago. Despite its lofty title, the Commission was managed and directed by a Chicago lawyer named Luis Kutner, who had also founded the organization. It was located in Kutner's law office, and its only source of income was from Kutner's pocket. It did have a tax exemption. Gorman and Edwards met with Kutner and offered him $7,500 a month in exchange for that tax exemption. Kutner agreed. In order to bring Friends of the FBI within the limits of the Commission's charter, Kutner was forced to characterize Friends as an "objective, unpredetermined" study of the FBI, thus creating a rather novel definition of friendship as well as of charity. But the big coup was obtaining for their first and only solicitation letter the endorsement of Mr. FBI himself, TV star Efrem Zimbalist, Jr. Zimbalist took out a few moments from a filming, signed a blank piece of paper, and authorized Lee Edwards to use it on the solicitation letter.

Launched in 1971, the direct-mail solicitation brought in close to four hundred thousand dollars in four months. Over two hundred thousand dollars was consumed in expenses. The rest was divided: about $140,000 for Gorman, $50,000 for Kutner, and the rest to Edwards. Zimbalist repudiated his endorsement. Lee Edwards says he is no longer connected with the enterprise. An FBI spokesperson angrily told me that the agency is checking into the possibility of preventing Gorman from using its name in this vein. Kutner recently wrote a letter to the District of Columbia License Bureau stating that the charitable-solicitation permit obtained for Friends of the FBI in the name of his Commission was obtained by "certain people in Washington" without his permission. However, Kutner does admit accepting that fifty thousand dollars.

To appreciate the full extent of Gorman's profits, it is important to understand the value of a good mailing list and the way such a list is developed. The mail solicitor is constantly striving to build and perfect a personal or "house" list of as many people as possible who are likely to respond favorably to a charitable appeal. For Gorman's lists, the ideal person is a political conservative who will rush to the checkbook in fear of the peaceniks or out of love for the Agnews. The only way to perfect such a list is to obtain and use as many outside lists as possible. You take the subscription list of a conservative magazine, and use it for the fundraising drive of Friends of the FBI or Americans for Agnew. The people who respond are placed on the Gorman house list. They have revealed their vulnerability. They have become targets of the next Gorman enterprise.

From this viewpoint, Gorman's risks are minimal. He can invest a small amount in a lukewarm fund-raising idea, use outside lists, and, even if he only breaks even or loses a little money, he has still gained enough new names for his house list to make it all worthwhile. Then, when a really super idea comes along, with a superstar like Zimbalist to endorse it, he can haul out his house lists, invest substantial sums of money in the campaign, and make a bundle. It makes charity promotion a tempting path for those who have the stomach for it. And it means that a lot of charity-solicitation letters that reach our mailboxes come not from full-fledged charitable organizations, but from the imaginations of charity promoters who operate in the name of profit (for a more complete discussion of direct-mail fund raising, see chapter 5).

The charity-promotion business was founded by Abraham Koolish. Koolish had been involved in several dubious business schemes before he entered the charity field. He had also been a person of considerable interest to the Federal Trade Commission (FTC), having attracted several FTC orders as a result of his ventures and a fine for violating one of those orders. During the early 1940s, American charity began attracting big money, and people like Abraham Koolish are always among the first to hop onto that kind of bandwagon. In 1943 Koolish entered into an arrangement with the Disabled American Veterans that set that organization on the path to becoming the least charitable major charity in America (See chapter 8). The arrangement also did Abraham Koolish quite a bit of good and set him on the path of becoming the most successful charity fraud in American history.

In his 1943 contract with the veterans' organization, Koolish agreed to conduct a mass mail fund-raising solicitation, enclosing in each letter a fund-raising gimmick called the ident-o-tag, a miniature replica of an automobile license plate. After raking in over a million dollars through this

contractual arrangement, Koolish sold the ident-o-tag gimmick to the Disabled American Veterans for another million-
plus and then went on to equally green charity pastures. He
set up the National Association of Veterans Employment
Councils—a group that raised over two million dollars in
less than two years, spent practically all of it on fund raising,
and then folded. He organized the National Kids' Day
Foundation, which somehow attracted the support of some
very respectable community organizations in cities throughout the nation. This supposedly charitable enterprise raised
over four million dollars in five years and spent 92 per cent
of this on fund raising and public relations, and the remain-
ing 8 per cent on future fund-raising projects. Most of this
money was paid to Gayton Associates, a fund-raising firm
owned by Abraham Koolish. National Kids' Day was forced
to close down after Bing Crosby and other high-powered
celebrities complained that their names were being used
without permission.

In 1949, Abraham Koolish launched an enterprise that
made his earlier golden eggs seem like tiny pebbles. It began
with a fund-raising contract between Koolish and the Sister
Kenny Institute, a charity devoted to treating polio patients.
It was a time when polio was the most popular charitable
cause in America, and Abraham Koolish was certainly an
expert at converting charitable causes, valid and otherwise,
to big money. Between 1951 and 1960, Koolish raised $22
million for the Kenny Institute. However, only $9 million of
that amount ever reached the organization and the polio
patients it was supposed to be serving. You see, Koolish
had reached a secret understanding with Marvin Kline,
former mayor of Minneapolis and executive director of the
Kenny Institute (located in Minneapolis). Pursuant to that
understanding, Koolish and Kline siphoned off most of the
contributions for themselves, hiding the millions they

pocketed under phony fund-raising and public-education expenditures.

In 1960, Senator Walter Mondale—then attorney general of Minnesota—exposed the scheme. Koolish and Kline were indicted and later convicted of mail fraud by a federal district court in Minneapolis. Each was sentenced to ten years in jail, their appeals denied. See *Koolish* v. *United States,* 340 Fed. 2d 513 (8th Cir., 1965). Don't let the ending of this tale mislead you. The Kline-Koolish conspiracy romped along successfully for eleven years and an estimated $16 million in profits. Had they stopped a little earlier or taken a little less, they would probably still be in business.

Full-time charity promotion is a delicate operation. The right associates must be cultivated and maintained. You have to do business through several entities and keep track of which is doing what, and when. Countless schemes have to be invented, evaluated, and effected. Mailing lists require constant attention. The most important thing is to stay in the background and keep moving. It is the organization, real or invented, that will be criticized first. Hopefully you will be undetectable behind a long row of business entities or long gone to other enterprises. This was the mistake of Abraham Koolish in the Kenny Institute conspiracy. He stayed too long and he was too visible. He undoubtedly knew better, but $16 million is a lot of money.

It adds up to a lot of energy, which many would-be charity promoters do not feel like investing. Some of them enter other business fields—usually those that border on the charity world—and engage in charity promotion as a sideline. A few years ago I developed a case study of just such a person—Leonard Stanley—the owner of a Washington printing firm who dabbled in charity during his spare time.

Leonard Stanley was engaged in several types of charity profiteering. He managed something called the Blind Artists

Concert, which raised $10,000 in two years and gave $6,000 of it to Stanley for his services, $1,500 to the artists, and the rest for expenses. He ran the Community Boys Club, an organization that tried to appear very much like the boy's club run by the District of Columbia police department, but which bore as much resemblance to that organization as does a hen to an antelope. Fund raising for the Stanley club was conducted by boys recruited from the streets of the inner city. Stanley's associate would drive the boys out to the suburbs and send them door to door selling candy at exorbitant prices in the name of charity. The kids were told to give false names if questioned by police. Many mothers were not advised where their boys were being taken or what they were doing. Proceeds from these solicitations were divided 50 per cent to Leonard Stanley, 25 per cent to L & C Associates (a company owned by Stanley), 20 per cent for advertising, and 5 per cent to the young solicitors.

As anyone who has a house in the suburbs well knows, profiteering in the name of charity takes many shapes in door-to-door merchandise solicitation. I remember a college friend, who worked his way through school selling encyclopedias, once telling me: "The worst part of it is when you just start out with a new company. You keep forgetting whether you're supposed to be a poor college kid who gets a prize for selling the most books or a rich college kid who's donating everything to the Red Cross." Of course, many of the people who succumb to the doorstep charity pitch are really not buying the Red Cross story. They think the person at the door is cute and they want to help that person, not some mythical cause. But, in a very real sense, the solicitor is indeed a charitable cause personified. And what most people fail to realize is that the money they "contribute" is going in substantial part to some business-for-profit, a business that is using cute college kids to con us into buying something we would not give a second glance in the marketplace. In this respect, there is very little difference between encyclopedia selling and the charity business.

Although charities are not-for-profit enterprises, they border directly on a vast conglomerate of businesses, legitimate and otherwise, that exist for the sole purpose of making money, in whole or in part by serving the charity world. In the Yellow Pages of every major city, there is a separate listing for "Fund Raising Organizations." Beneath that heading are listed consultants and public-relations people. There are firms that specialize in printing and artwork for charitable organizations. There are producers and venders of all those trinkets that are "sold" to charitable contributors. There are also caterers who can "make your fundraising banquets and receptions truly memorable occasions." On and on. But even all these make up only a sliver of that business conglomerate. Stationery, office supplies, legal and accounting services, office space—all come to charities by way of businesses that profit from the charitable dollar. Oftentimes a charity must turn to one of these businesses as the only supplier of true necessities. In other cases, while the services and supplies may not be absolutely needed, their acquisition is perfectly reasonable and beneficial to the charity and its cause. On the other hand, there are some very large and very real dangers in this aspect of the charity business, particularly when coupled with those biblical myths.

BENEFIT CONCERT! CHARITY GAME! PROCEEDS TO CHARITY! In some cases, such as the Concert for Bangladesh, the performers and participants do indeed donate their time and talent, and various other essentials are donated without charge. But in many of these situations, probably the majority, a lot of people are planning to make a lot of money from the event. And they do. Sometimes the promoter is just another Abraham Koolish, using the name of charity to fill his own pockets at our expense. But even the legitimate charity functions often wind up dishing out only a few crumbs to charity because of all the profits that eat away at receipts.

Take a football charity exhibition game, for example. Before one penny of the gate receipts reaches charity, the owner of the football stadium gets his rent. Part of that rent is profit. How the rest of the receipts are divided depends on the contract between the two professional teams and the charitable organization. The contract usually provides that the teams get first cut of net receipts up to a certain amount, dividing the remainder with the charity. In a typical arrangement, the teams split the first $80,000 in net receipts, everything above this being divided into thirds, the charitable organization receiving one portion. Part of the $40,000-plus received by each team is, of course, profit. If net receipts happen to fall below $80,000, the charity gets nothing. There are similar arrangements behind charity circuses. And for many benefit concerts, the performers charge their full rates for making an appearance.

This is not intended as criticism of the circus performers, football players, and rock stars who participate in these events. They have a right to whatever they can earn for risking their necks on the high wire, getting clobbered on a football field, or grinding away for hours before a screaming audience. Furthermore, they usually have nothing to do with whether an event is characterized as a benefit performance or as an enterprise for profit. Similarly, the owners of football stadiums and circus arenas cannot be expected to operate their facilities for the sake of charity. And football-team owners might well argue that they should be commended for sharing at least some of their profits with charitable enterprises.

The problem is that no one lets us in on the contractual

arrangements behind the charity events we are asked to patronize. We are shown a worthy cause and offered a ticket. We are not told how many people will profit from the ticket price before the cause sees even one penny. In most cases, no one actually tries to mislead us. But we see the word "charity" and we believe the ancient tales that have been so carefully preserved for our benefit.

Contrary to the grand illusion, our non-profit charity system is shot through with opportunity for profit. A research grant can go to the executive director's nephew, who spends it all on a fully carpeted laboratory and a beautiful lab assistant. A third of an organization's printing costs may be exorbitant profits of a firm that treated the chief executive to a Bahamas vacation. A good part of a charity's budget may consist of fabricated and unneeded projects, concocted to keep the organization in business and its employees in the money. The same people and attitudes that brought us the oil-depletion allowance, the American Dream, and the sharp business practice can just as easily create similar monsters in the charity business. It means that there is no automatic pilot set on an unswerving philanthropic course. Rather, charity is a system subject to the influence of conflicting vested interests, some of which are very uncharitable indeed.

The two most obvious and justifiable charity interest groups are the contributors and the recipients. The contributors want a charity system that will give them full value for their money. The recipients want a system that will deliver as much of that money as possible where it is really needed (which is actually pretty much what the contributors have in mind). The charity recipients, however, are totally disenfranchised people. They are the ones who write letters to their congressman complaining about the elevators in the Gerbitz Building being too small for wheelchairs, while their

congressman is having dinner with Gerbitz. Put them in any
system you like, and they will have zero impact on it. Of
course, it is an entirely different matter with the contributors. They control the purse strings. But the interest of the
American contributor seldom extends past the checkbook.

There is, as we have seen, another group with a vested
interest in our charity system. It is composed of all the people and groups who can profit from the charitable dollar.
They run the gamut from the print shop around the corner
to the Abraham Koolishes. They include the pop singer with
five "benefit" performances each year, the charity executive
(with or without a nephew), the consultant, the office supplier, and the trinket maker. Most of these people are
shrewd and hard. They know how to protect their interests
and keep things just as nice as they are.

In other American systems in which powerful vested interests work contrary to social needs and purposes, we at
least make some effort to counterbalance the impact of those
interests. This is what our Founding Fathers had in mind
when they devised a three-branch government and a Bill of
Rights. Perfection we certainly do not have. But at least the
public interest has some representation. As we shall now see,
the charity system is quite a bit different.

4   Regulation: The Big Sleep

Effective regulation of a particular system in the public interest requires laws prescribing proper conduct, authority to enforce those laws, and people who use that authority wisely and energetically. In all three respects, regulation of American charity is practically non-existent.

A notion of considerable popularity among people I encounter is that the federal government, primarily through the Internal Revenue Service, stands as an eternal and omnipotent watchdog against all abuses in the charity business. I do not know whether this belief is the result of wishful thinking or one of the charity myths perpetrated with premeditated design on the American public. But whatever the cause, the notion is unsupported by reality. For one thing, the authority is lacking. The law empowers the IRS to grant and rescind tax exemptions, and this immediately eliminates from the scope of IRS charity regulation those organizations that do not apply for tax exemptions (although they are, of course, still subject to IRS authority over tax evaders and such).

None of Leonard Stanley's enterprises bothered to apply for exemptions. The Rudy Brothers Circus travels from city to city and, in exchange for a $10,000 payment to a charitable organization, obtains the organization's permission to use its name in telephone solicitations. The circus has its own telephone solicitors, who work around the clock trying to sell tickets in the name of charity. It does not apply for a tax exemption.

As for charitable organizations that do request exemptions, the IRS first determines whether the organization has a charitable purpose. If so, the organization gets a tax exemption. Under provisions of the Internal Revenue Code, an organization does not have a "charitable purpose" if it engages in lobbying or political-campaign activities to a substantial extent or if it is set up in such a way that its profits benefit the people who control the organization. This does not preclude the people in control from awarding themselves salaries or consultant fees. Once a tax exemption is granted, the IRS is empowered to audit the organization and determine whether its stated purpose is being carried out. If it is not, the exemption can be rescinded and the organization be required to pay taxes on its activities retroactively. If the IRS discovers that false information was given on informational returns, it can recommend that the people involved be prosecuted criminally for giving false information under oath to a government official.

This leaves some rather large loopholes in IRS authority over charitable organizations. There is no provision in the law that empowers the IRS to take action against profiteering through ludicrous fund-raising costs, exorbitant salaries, or overinflated consultant fees. There is no restriction against forming your own charity and paying yourself to raise money for it. There is no requirement that an organization's "charitable purpose" fill a valid social need or be more than a mere flight of fancy, or an invention to serve a fundraising enterprise. There is no prohibition against creating a paper organization and then pulling fly-by-night enterprises under its umbrella. The case histories set out in the previous chapter are clear evidence of what the law does allow. Those dubious enterprises throve. Most of them operated with the benefit of an IRS tax exemption.

America has, however, known more than one regulatory agency that took an activist approach to legislated responsibility and converted skimpy laws to effective enforcement tools. A notable example is the recent transformation of the Federal Trade Commission from pussycat to tiger in the area of deceptive advertising. It did this by broadening its own views of its authority and hoping that the courts would agree. So far, this approach has proved successful. The IRS could certainly do the same. We could reasonably argue, for example, that a charitable organization that has been eating up millions of dollars each year for ten years without benefiting its charitable cause is not really being operated for a charitable purpose. We could say that a fund-raising contract that guarantees the people running a charity more money than can possibly be raised is a thinly disguised method of obtaining the organization's net profits for the use of those in charge. The IRS does not say these things.

The primary reason is more practical than philosophical. It would be foolish for an agency to take a broader view of its responsibilities if it lacked the funds and staff to enforce its expanded authority. Such is the case with the IRS. It has its hands full, not only with income tax and similar matters, but also with an intensive five-year audit of every private foundation in the nation—a monumental task. To obtain the additional budget and staff for active regulation of charitable organizations, the agency would first have to convince a significant number of officeholders, in both the executive and the legislative branches of government, that the American public needs protection against American charity. And then, of course, the officeholders would have to convince their constituents that all those myths are lies.

There is no guarantee that the IRS officials are themselves immune from the myths. "It's my impression that if we audited all major charities, we wouldn't find much," one told me during an informal chat. "Oh, I know there are a few shady operators. But we can't do everything. We have to hope that the prosecutors will be able to deal with them. But the major organizations are all on the up-and-up. Aren't they?"

The prosecutors have their own problems. In order to take action against a fraudulent charity, the fraud has to be uncovered, in the first place. Prosecuting attorneys have plenty to do without going outside their offices or the courtroom. They certainly do not have the time to dig around among IRS returns or sift through annual reports of charitable organizations. This means that a charity fraud must be called to the attention of a prosecutor by a complaining member of the public. Who will complain? A contributor who neither seeks nor receives information on how the charitable organization spends its contributions? A trustee whose reputation will be tarnished if the organization becomes involved in a horrid scandal? Perhaps. But not very likely and not very often.

Even if a heinous act by a charity promoter or fund raiser or executive is somehow uncovered, no one will be prosecuted unless that act is illegal as well as shocking. The two go hand in hand in very few instances. It is not illegal to organize a charity and pay yourself enormous sums from its coffers. It is not necessarily illegal to raise money for a cause that receives not a penny you raise. What is illegal in most jurisdictions is obtaining money from contributors with the intention of committing fraud—that is, intentionally deceiving the public for the purpose of obtaining other people's money for your own private use.

It is not an easy thing to prove when it comes to charities. In the business world, you pay money only in exchange for some product or service. If you are deceived as to the value of the product or the nature of the service, the proof is either in your hand or in your testimony. What can you say about a charity? Patrick Gorman does not assure you that every penny you contribute will go to his cause, and he certainly doesn't guarantee you a particular result. He may not tell you how much of your dollar will benefit him, but which charity does disclose its fund-raising costs during a solicitation?

"That's one of the main problems," a prosecuting attorney once told me. "You either have to say that they're all committing larceny or none of them are. Of course, it's a different story if you can prove that they actually intended to deceive their contributors and pocket everything they raised themselves. But you can't just open up a person's mind and present it to the jury. And don't forget, we're not talking about automatic transmission companies. We're talking about CHARITIES! They're going to sit back in court and tell the jury about all the wonderful things they'll do for

America as soon as they get their young organization off the ground. Do you have any idea what would happen if we brought that kind of case and lost it? The next day, every crook in town would be forming his own charity."

People who commit charity fraud and other white-collar crimes are usually very much aware of what their fellow white-collar criminals are doing and how they are being treated by the law enforcers and the courts. There is indeed a very real danger of encouraging more charity fraud by prosecuting a tenuous case. Equally important, judges are generally reluctant to impose heavy sentences on people who commit non-street crimes. Someone who bathes regularly and goes to the right country club stands a good chance of receiving a suspended sentence in exchange for a solemn promise never to do it again. Of course, such a result can have the same encouraging effect as an outright defeat for the prosecution.

We can find further reason to excuse the regulators and prosecutors in the fact that there is very definitely a line beyond which regulation of the charity business becomes dangerous for the public, that line being much clearer and closer than it is for other business systems. A pet principle of people and interests that do not want to be regulated is that regulation means control. The danger is certainly minimal when applied to massive corporations that can buy off government officials without wincing, and do. But there is indeed a selective process in regulation and law enforcement. There has to be. You cannot audit and prosecute everyone. And since charity is a world of ideas as well as of money, there is a great danger that prosecuting attorneys and government regulators will allow their political views and personal prejudices to overinfluence which charities they select as dangerous to the public. I would not have wanted Richard Kleindienst determining whether an environmental group or the Fund for Investigative Journalism spends too much on fund raising or devotes its resources to valid purposes.

In other areas, when the government demonstrates a lack of energy in defending the public against victimizing enterprises, there are opportunities for private estates—perhaps the victims themselves—to act. If General Motors turns out a dangerous line of automobiles, the threat of millions of dollars in damage suits is a greater inducement for corrective action than the snail-like machinery of the Department of Transportation or a possible consent order (I didn't do it, but I won't do it again) induced by the Federal Trade Commission. We are, in fact, witnessing the development of the civil court action into one of the most potent public weapons in America. Not so in the charity world.

Much of the problem is legal. Since contributors neither expect nor receive anything in exchange for the money they donate unconditionally to a charity, they are really not damaged in a legal sense when the charity fails to make good use of their money. The same reasoning applies to charity recipients, who have no legal right to anything that a charitable organization gives them—or should give them. There is also the requirement that a plaintiff must have a substantial interest in the subject matter of a suit, which may be a bit difficult to establish as one of a million contributors to a particular organization. But it is despite such barricades that new legal concepts and new social policies are conceived.

As far as I know, not one potential contributor in this country has tested his right to full information from a charity he wishes to support, or from one he has already supported. Perhaps there is a legal right—not yet proclaimed—to be fully informed about our charities so we can freely and intelligently decide where to contribute. Perhaps the courts would agree with the idea that there is an implied condition behind every charitable donation: reasonable use of the charitable dollar. Perhaps a farseeing and understanding judge would conceive of a way to set out reasonable safeguards for contributors without overburdening legitimate charity functions. There is no way to know these things; no one is testing these possibilities.

One group was founded many decades ago to serve the American contributor. This is the National Information Bureau (NIB), a membership association that provides its members with reports on charitable organizations. There are several problems: Its staff is small. It has no way to obtain information from an uncooperative charity. It must often rely on estimates and secondhand statistics. Most important, the NIB has its own fish to fry. When the NIB learned that I was writing this book, it refused to admit me as a member, and it refused my repeated requests to discuss its activities and the charity system. "We are on the same side, we can help each other," I said to the NIB. "We are competitors, you might put us out of business," I was told by the NIB. It seems rather strange conduct for an organization dedicated to educating and protecting contributors.

When a friend of mine heard that I was writing a book on charities, she telephoned to advise me that she was an NIB member and to ask whether I wanted to see the NIB reports she had retained. I accepted the offer and she sent me forty-two reports. They each dealt with a charity in which my friend was interested. With one or two exceptions, the organizations are well known. Since each report is labeled "confidential," I will not reveal the names of the organizations. The reports follow a pattern. They begin with a general discussion of the organization, a financial statement, some specific comments, and a conclusion.

Among the reports I received, I found three types of NIB

conclusions. In some cases, the contributor is advised that the organization meets NIB standards or that the NIB sees no reason why the contributor should not support the organization. In other cases, the contributor is warned that the organization does not meet NIB standards. Finally, the NIB may advise the contributor that it has not conducted a study of the organization sufficient to reach any conclusion at all. Of the forty-two reports sent to me, the NIB concluded that eighteen of the organizations were acceptable and that three of the organizations were not acceptable. In exactly half of the reports, the NIB did not reach any conclusion at all. But, in some of these cases, the report includes some comments that can be helpful to a contributor.

The general discussion section is somewhat sketchy, but certainly better than no information at all. Most of the financial statements reveal cost items such as salaries and postage without allocating such costs among program and supporting services. In my view, this is a rather meaningless method of financial disclosure for charities, since it does not tell us how employee time was spent or to what purpose the postage and printing were devoted. In most of the forty-two cases, I would be unable to make an intelligent decision without first obtaining an annual report.

The NIB reports do contain some information that we would not find in an annual report. For example, many NIB reports reveal the number of times the board of trustees has met during the year. Some tell us what the organization's top executives receive for their services. Finally, we occasionally find the views of the NIB staff on a particular type of charity or on a fund-raising method employed by a particular organization. Since NIB members can request as many reports as the NIB publishes, since the reports do contain some useful information, and since the cost to a contributor is only fifteen dollars annually (as of this writing),

NIB membership seems worth the price. At the same time, it would be very unwise to contribute solely on the basis of the reports I have seen.

The Council of Better Business Bureaus has opened a two-person office in Washington which investigates and reports on charitable solicitations. I have spoken to both people in the office and reviewed the material they have published. The people seem well intentioned and they have done a good job of pinpointing several fringe charity operations. But they are only two people. And they are being paid by the Better Business Bureau. Whether by accident or design, the Bureau has sometimes done a lot more to protect our business crooks than their victims—handing out honest-business membership plaques to some of our most blatant frauds, neglecting to publicize complaints about Better Business Bureau members, and otherwise doing an imperfect job of policing the profession that brought us the auto-transmission fraud, the dance-studio racket, and the Holland Furnace Company game. During an hour-long interview, one of the people in the Bureau's charitable-solicitations office demonstrated the usual Bureau approach to consumer protection by dodging questions on atrocities committed by our "reputable" charities (those with Better Business Bureau members on their boards). "Well, they've had some problems," was the usual reply. We have bigger problems.

In January 1972, Representative Lionel Van Deerlin (D., California) received an inquiry from one of his constituents who had been asked to contribute to the Underground Bible Fund and wanted to know whether it was a worthwhile charity. Van Deerlin's administrative assistant, Siegmund Smith, undertook an investigation. He discovered that the Bible Fund had no telephone listing. He went to the address provided on the solicitation letter. A woman an-

swered the door and said she was not the Underground
Bible Fund. She told Smith that she had made an arrangement to accept and hold mail addressed to the charity, and
that a man stopped by periodically to pick up that mail.
She said that the man's name was Lee Edwards.

Further inquiries by Smith revealed that the Bible Fund's
only fund raiser was Patrick Gorman, that most of the
money raised was spent on fund raising, and that Gorman
does not like to give out information on his activities. Outraged, Smith and Van Deerlin immediately set to work
drafting legislation that would have required all charitable
solicitors to advise potential contributors as to how much of
their contributions would be going for a charitable purpose.
Van Deerlin sent the proposed bill to fund raisers and
charity executives. Then the trouble began.

The charity people descended on Van Deerlin's office.
They congratulated him on taking such a bold step in the
public interest and they offered their suggestions. They
pointed out how dangerous it would be to come right out
and hit contributors with the facts about fund raising, and
how could they accurately estimate how much they would
raise and spend, and maybe they should all get together
and draw up a really workable bill. So a committee of fund
raisers and charity executives was formed. One of the Better
Business Bureau charity-solicitations people was included on
the committee. They came up with a tentative revision
which, if passed, would simply require an organization
conducting a direct-mail solicitation to advise potential contributors that financial information is available upon request and to comply with such a request *if* the request is
made within a reasonable time and *if* a stamped return envelope is included along with the request.

As matters now stand, we are free to write to our
favorite charity and request an annual report without en-

closing a stamped envelope. If it is a reputable organization that has some concern for our welfare, it will send us meaningful information on its financial and other activities. Failure to do this provides us with a valuable clue about the nature of the organization we have been supporting. But under the charity committee's proposed legislation, an organization would be empowered by law to ignore our request unless we enclosed a stamped envelope and made the request within a reasonable time of a charitable solicitation, whatever that means. Moreover, the charity committee's proposal could not be more vague about what an organization is required to tell us. There is no provision for uniform accounting and reporting methods. There is no definition setting out the meaning of fund-raising costs, public-education costs, and similar items.

Behind the proposed legislation is a depressing attitude: a dedication to keeping us in the dark at all costs, a resolve to defeat any meaningful attempt to pry open the sealed lips and closed doors of the charity world. At this writing, Van Deerlin has not agreed to introduce the proposed legislation. Hopefully, he will refuse to do the American contributor so great a disservice.

There is little more to say about governmental regulation of charities. There are a few state and local governments with charity disclosure laws, but here we too often run into those unexplainable exemptions for veterans' organizations and such. More often than that, we find a complete lack of interest, energy, and direction. The District of Columbia has a law that requires any organization soliciting in the area first to apply for a permit and, after the solicitation ends, to file a financial statement. Neither Patrick Gorman nor Leonard Stanley encountered any difficulty in obtaining permits for their various enterprises. In fact, an official at the District of Columbia License

Bureau responsible for issuing such permits once told me that he has no authority to deny a permit to anyone.

"Do you mean to tell me that a convicted felon could walk in here, tell you he's forming a charity and that he intends to put every penny he raises into his pocket, and you would have to give him a permit to conduct a charitable solicitation?"

"That's right."

There is authority to deny a permit to a previous permit holder who failed to file a financial statement after a solicitation. Patrick Gorman has never filed a financial statement for any of the enterprises I have uncovered. He has never been denied a permit.

"It's a license to steal," a prosecutor told me. "Just put yourself in my place. We get a beautiful case of charity fraud against someone. So he comes into court, admits everything and hauls out his solicitation permit. 'How can it be illegal?' he says to the judge. 'I told them what I was going to do and the government gave me a license to do it.' If you were me, would you prosecute a case like that?"

There is no Uniform Commercial Code to protect contributors to charitable organizations. There is no Federal Trade Commission guarding the public against deceptive charity advertising. There is no magazine you can read that will tell you which charities are good investments this year. There is no consumer group using the law to rip open the charity system and bring it in line with the public interest. We are naked, defenseless. We are forced to hope that there are sufficient safeguards within that closed business system to protect our interests. But are there?

5   Fund Raising:
The Rules of the Game

I have a friend who takes great delight in the deflation of
sacred cows. When I told him I was writing a book on
charities, he was very pleased. "It's that chapter on fund
raising I want to see," he told me, wringing his hands in
gleeful villainy. I was not surprised. I had heard it at
cocktail parties and read it in magazine articles. Fund
raising is charity's Armageddon. Here is where all the
atrocities occur, where all the fraud, extravagance, and
wastefulness join hands to form one gigantic contributor
rip-off. Thus comes the popular notion that the acid test of

a charity's worth is the amount of money it spends to raise more money. There is even a magic formula: fund-raising costs should not exceed 25 per cent of a charity's receipts. No one seems to know where it comes from. But the Civil Service Commission has given it governmental sanction by allowing only those charities that meet such a standard to solicit contributions from government employees. So, the thinking goes, in order to locate a good charity, we need only look at its fund-raising costs. If they are below the 25 per cent standard, we should have no qualms about sending in a donation. It seems so obvious and natural. Those are the two things that bother me.

We are dealing with a closed system, a system that is not at all eager to publicize meaningful information about itself. How did this wonderful formula, this priceless aid to the American contributor, slip under the door so easily? In another of our closed systems—the political one—there is a concoction known as a red herring. Unlike a dead herring, such a thing cannot be detected by odor. In fact, the real clue to a red herring is its absence of smell. It seems so obvious and natural that we wonder how we missed it before.

A second clue is that this obvious truth just happens to serve the best interests of the people who control the system. Popular notions about charitable fund raising do indeed serve the charity system, and in two ways: first, they focus public attention on only one phase of an organization's operation, and second, they provide a definite standard for the charity to meet in order to satisfy public opinion. And the nature of the charity business certainly allows an organization to meet that standard on paper, regardless of what it actually spends on fund raising.

The major expense item in nearly every charity's budget is salaries. The total amount that an organization pays to

its employees is, for reporting purposes, allocated over its
various activities in accordance with the time each employee devotes to each activity. In some cases, an employee
spends every working minute of the year on a single program, and his or her entire salary is allocated to that
program. Most employees, however, divide their time
among several programs and also engage in fund raising
and general management activities. At the end of the year,
the employee makes out a little form estimating the amount
of time devoted to each activity. Place yourself in that
employee's chair. Remember: high fund-raising costs are
to be avoided at all costs, and high anything-else is perfectly
all right. So you slant your estimates away from fund
raising. The comptroller cranks your estimate in with the
others and, alas, the fund-raising total still comes out 30
per cent. The telephone rings.

"We don't want to question your judgment, but we
were wondering about that Dallas trip you listed under
fund raising. Is that all you did down there?"

"Well, no. I visited the chapter office to say hello."

"Ahhhh. Community Services."

According to the 1971 annual report of the National
Foundation (March of Dimes), the organization raised $26.6
million that year and spent it as follows:

1. Fund Raising .... $5.7 million
2. Patient Services .... $5.5 million
3. Research .... $4.4 million
4. Public Education .... $3.9 million
5. Community Services .... $3.4 million
6. Management .... $2.1 million
7. Professional Education ...... $1.3 million

If we accept these figures, fund raising works out to 22 per
cent of receipts, respectably within the rule-of-thumb for-

mula. But $8 million—nearly one third—of National Foundation expenditures was paid out in salaries and employee benefits. And an interesting thing happens when we check into how the organization's employees estimated their time for the 1971 report:

1. Public Education .... $2 million
2. Community Services .... $1.9 million
3. Fund Raising .... $1.4 million
4. Management .... $1.3 million
5. Patient Services $700,000
6. Professional Education $500,000
7. Research Support $150,000

A major result of the organization's Public Education program is the pile of literature I obtained during a visit to the Foundation's Washington office. Except for one booklet on prenatal care, every item of literature in my possession is devoted one third to health care and two thirds to educating the reader on the National Foundation and its dedication to fighting birth defects. If two thirds of the public-education budget were allocated to fund raising, fund-raising costs would zoom to over 30 per cent of receipts.

The National Foundation is certainly not the only charity in America that may be fudging on fund-raising estimates.[1]

"I don't give a damn what they say on their financial statements," a charity executive told me (after a couple of drinks). "With very few exceptions, there is no way they can raise money as cheaply as they say they do. And by exceptions, I'm talking about Cancer and Heart and

---

[1] Actually, the National Foundation should be commended for publishing sufficiently detailed information on its expenditures to make a meaningful analysis of fund-raising costs possible.

maybe one or two others that can get a contribution just by holding out a hand. The rest of them are spending a third and more on fund raising and hiding it under Public Education or Community Services."

There is no proof that such things are actually done. We cannot hold a stop watch to charity employees. At the same time, the opportunity for deceit clearly exists. And there is no denying that, in light of the public focus on fund raising, the temptation to deceive us is great.

There are other reasons for believing that fund raising is a very unreliable barometer of a charity's worth. Foremost among these is the fact that more and more of today's charities have abandoned such traditional fundraising methods as telethons, benefit concerts, and door-to-door campaigning, and have turned to direct-mail solicitation instead.

It is a deceptively simple way to raise money. All you need is a stamped envelope, a solicitation letter, perhaps a trinket like the Koolish indent-o-tag, and someone to send it all to. But what do you say in the letter? Should you use expensive paper (they might think you're being extravagant) or cheap paper (they might think you're a fly-by-night)? Should you use bright colors, a lot of photographs? What about celebrity endorsements? Should you hire a direct-mail consultant (they can be very expensive) or try it on your own (that can be very foolhardy)? Then there is the question of mailing lists.

If you open any issue of *Fund Raising Management* magazine, you will find advertisements for all types of lists. In the February 1972 issue is an ad by Dependable Mailing Lists, Incorporated: "325,000 conservative minded individuals, List ⚡114, @$25.00 per M; 158,000 liberal minded individuals, List ⚡104, @$25.00 per M." Most people in the direct-mail field will tell you that the only decent way to determine the money-raising potential of a particular mailing list is to do a test run of at least ten thousand names. That means $250 for list rental, $800 for postage, and enough time, printing, and stationery to bring your initial investment to over three thousand dollars, perhaps as high as five or six thousand dollars. Are you going to risk that kind of money on ten thousand liberals you have never seen? Or should you try some of the "168,000 Protestants" offered by the Fund Raising Marketing Company, or a few of the "80,000 women buyers of Hill Brothers shoes" that Mosely Mail Order will rent to you for $30 per thousand names?

Direct-mail solicitation is a very delicate operation, requiring just the right combination of material, solicitation approach, and mailing lists. Even for the experts, it is a chancy business. For the novice, it is an outright gamble, and a very expensive gamble at that. At the same time, a direct-mail solicitation can click into a monetary landslide of awesome proportions. But this kind of success does not at all mean that the charitable organization conducting the solicitation deserves the money.

The "direct" is really a misnomer. In no other form of fund raising is the organization so removed from the potential contributor. There is no in-the-flesh campaigner for us to evaluate or question. The celebrities who endorse the campaign are not required to prove their commitment by sacrificing a few hours of time, and circumstance does not force those celebrities to work with the charity executives and get to know what the organization has been doing. The success of Patrick Gorman's Friends of the FBI was due in great part to a solicitation letter signed by TV star Efrem Zimbalist, Jr. Zimbalist signed a blank slip of paper and give it to Gorman associate Lee Edwards. The signature was later reproduced beneath the letter written by Gorman. Zimbalist did not read the letter. Nor did he investigate the organization he was endorsing. He later repudiated his endorsement, but only after Gorman had raked in close to $500,000 from Zimbalist fans.

Adding to the gap between the charity and its contributors is the amount of contrivance and mechanical manipulation involved in a direct-mail solicitation. All we see is a letter that has been rewritten and tested countless times by the public-relations and direct-mail people. Various types of colors, printing styles, and written texts are tried, abandoned, and tried again. If the campaign is successful, it may well be much less a tribute to the worthiness of the organization than to the technical skill of its employees and consultants. Or the success may be purely accidental —someone stumbles across a productive mailing list, or the right pitch at the right time.

The cause is the thing in charitable fund raising. Not only does a good cause fail to guarantee a decent organization behind it, but a cause that can attract massive public support is not necessarily a good cause. This is particularly true in direct-mail fund raising, through which you can deliver a quick emotional punch and direct it at groups of people you know will be most vulnerable to it, because of the magazines they read, the credit cards they use, the politicians they rally around, or the stores they patronize. In direct-mail fund raising, the actual nature of an organization's cause is unimportant. The only thing that really matters is what that cause appears to be on paper.

In the health field, for example, a potential contributor must be made to believe that a disease is a very real personal threat of frightening proportions and that there is a reasonable chance of coming up with a cure for the disease. Although heart disease strikes fourteen times as many people as does cancer and claims four times as many lives, it does not seem as painful a malady or as readily curable. Thus, the American Cancer Society has been able to convert its cause into a much greater fund-raising success than that of the American Heart Association (in 1972, $84 million and $56 million respectively). Most Americans refuse to acknowledge that some of our most horrible diseases even exist—venereal disease, sickle-cell anemia, leprosy—and organizations dedicated to fighting such maladies do very poorly in fund raising.

A key element in direct-mail fund raising is the ease with which an organization can locate people who will respond graciously to a particular cause. Just by staying in business a long time, a charitable organization will acquire a large following of faithful supporters who, each year, respond reflexively and generously to the charity's appeal. An old organization is not necessarily a worthy organization. And an organization that was worthy yesterday is not necessarily worthy today. With some types of causes, it is much less difficult to locate groups of people who are apt to be responsive. The success of many charity promoters is founded on the fact that they solicit primarily through politically conservative causes. As a general rule, political conservatives are more wealthy than their liberal counterparts; more willing and able to support their favorite causes with money. There are enough subscribers to conservative magazines, contributors to conservative politicians, and members of conservative organizations —all identified on available mailing lists—to eliminate a great deal of the hit-and-miss element from red-white-and-blue fund raising. Charities that appeal to particular religious groups will, for the same reason, generally do better in fund raising than organizations that appeal to the general public.

Some organizations increase their fund-raising success

and reduce attendant costs by employing dubious methods, which most charities would reject out of hand. Take the Liberty Lobby, for example, an ultraconservative political-action group headquartered in Washington. Under the expert guidance of Willis A. Carto, the Liberty Lobby managed to build one of the most envied mailing lists in the conservative fund-raising field. It accomplished this by maintaining a respectable façade for itself and, at the same time, forming several extremist front groups for solicitation purposes.

While the Lobby appealed for funds in the name of political conservatism, the Friends of Rhodesian Independence—a secret Lobby offshoot—solicited potential contributors with blatantly racist literature. The *American Mercury* magazine, once the pride of H. L. Mencken, was acquired by the Liberty Lobby through a maze of interrelationships and began to publish anti-Semitic articles. In these ways, the Liberty Lobby mounted anti-busing, prosegregationist, and anti-Semitic fund-raising campaigns. Some of the appeals wound up in the red (figuratively speaking, of course!) and others were successful. But they all produced more names for the Liberty Lobby mailing list—people who could be relied upon to respond to the next Liberty Lobby solicitation. And they all served as a massive testing ground for new fund-raising techniques.

An interesting footnote to this story is that in April 1970 Louis Byers, president of still another Liberty Lobby offshoot (the National Youth Alliance), and Michael Russell, a Liberty Lobby employee, made off with that magnificent mailing list and began renting it to conservative fund raisers and pocketing the proceeds themselves. Their chief mailing-list broker was a man named Donald Phillips, another former Lobby employee, who had gone into business for himself with Heritage Advertising, a fund-raising outfit, and several pseudo charities. Michael Russell testified in a court deposition: "Mr. Phillips said he wanted 20 per cent, which is the normal fee for brokering. He told us he had a great many outlets, one of them being Mr. Gorman. He said that he and Gorman, he rented Gorman's files and Gorman rented his lists, so he had a great many outlets. You see, Gorman brokered his lists and he would broker Gorman's lists." Gorman? Not Patrick J. Gorman. Yes, indeed. The Liberty Lobby filed suit against Phillips and several of his associates (still pending at this writing). Russell and Byers had a falling out, after which they confessed their caper to Liberty Lobby attorneys and went their separate ways—Russell to a mundane job in Buffalo, New York, vowing never to engage in conservative fund raising again, and Byers to new fund-raising ventures, in partnership with William Pierce, of the American Nazi Party.

Fund-raising statistics alone do not tell us whether an organization has been dealing in front groups and pirated mailing lists, or whether its employees have been underestimating the time they devote to fund-raising activities, or whether the charity has been misleading its contributors into believing that its disease is more frightening or its cause is more worthy than it actually is. The statistics do not reveal whether the charity's fund-raising success was due to fluke, deceit, a talented consultant, a productive mailing list, or an efficient organization and truly worthwhile purpose. In fact, fund-raising statistics tell us very little about whether an organization is really a good charity investment. To be sure, an organization that spends most of the money it takes in on fund raising should not be applauded. And it is probably unworthy of our contributions, perhaps even an outright fraud. On the other hand, it may be a young organization that is dedicated to a very unpopular cause and doing the best it can under the circumstances.

Beneath the statistics are too many matters that are too important to ignore. Most of them concern the quality of a charity's fund-raising campaign, rather than its result. For example, many charitable organizations employ solicitors who are paid on a commission basis. This may be an effective way for some groups to raise money, but it is a terribly dangerous practice from the point of view of the contributor. It encourages solicitors to engage in misrepresentation, arm twisting, and who knows what else, in order to increase the amount of contributions they take in and the commissions they receive as a result.

Another dubious fund-raising practice is the sending of unordered merchandise to potential contributors. There can be only one motive behind such a fund-raising technique: to force upon a potential contributor a sense of obligation to contribute, which is of course, a very uncharitable thing for a charity to do. The American Veterans of World War II, Korean War and Viet Nam (AMVETS), a Congressionally chartered veterans' organization, has carried the merchandise solicitation even further. Targets of AMVETS direct-mail solicitation have received various types of gifts from the organization—neckties, Christmas cards, trinkets. Some of those who did not feel obligated to make a contribution eventually received a bill from the organization, demanding payment for the unordered merchandise.

In 1972 the American Kidney Fund—no relation to the National Kidney Foundation—raised a total of $779,434 through direct-mail solicitation and spent $604,000 of that amount on fund raising alone. But this tells only a very small part of the story. The president of the Fund, Swen Larsen, is also an incorporator of the Response Development Corporation, which holds an exclusive three-year fund-raising contract with Larsen's charity. Larsen told me that he no longer holds an interest in Response Development. But he admitted that this fund-raising firm is run by a close friend of his, John Swain. And he also admitted that a second Swain company, Mail Response Corporation, holds another three-year exclusive contract with the American Kidney Fund, this one for direct-mail services.

These are extreme examples, of course. But in order to shrug them off, we must first find a way to distinguish similar tales that come from the mainstream of American charity. During the late 1950s, for example, the part-time executive director of the American Cancer Society's Massachusetts Division was a man named James V. Lavin. Lavin devoted the rest of his working time to the James V. Lavin Company, a fund-raising firm owned by him. For his Cancer Society work, he received an annual salary of $17,500—not exactly a small piece of change for part-time work, particularly in those days. But this was not all. The best and steadiest client of Lavin's fund-raising firm was, yes, the Massachusetts Division of the American Cancer Society, from which Lavin received an annual fund-raising fee of $10,000. After several years of this cozy relationship, the arrangement was discovered and denounced by a public-spirited Cancer Society supporter. Lavin agreed to divest himself of all interest in the fund-raising firm, and he was rewarded with a full-time position at the Cancer Society at an annual salary of $25,000. But the fund-raising firm remained in operation, continuing to serve its best client. After Lavin's departure, the firm acquired a new employee: Saul Naglin. During the same period, the comptroller of the Massachusetts Division of the American Cancer Society was a man named, yes, Saul Naglin.

Through the late 1960s, the executive director of the Boys' Athletic League—a respected charity that runs summer camps for underprivileged youths in the New York area—was a man named Willard Kauth. His salary from the League was $26,000 annually. But this was not his only income from the charity business. He was also the general manager of the Girls Vacation Fund, for which he received an annual salary of $16,000. His wife happened to be the executive director of that charity. He also owned Donard, Incorporated, a fund-raising firm that had been used by both the Boys' Athletic League and the Girls Vacation Fund. Many of the fund-raising expenses that Donard charged off to its clients arose as a result of work done by a second firm—Noddra, Incorporated— which Donard hired on a regular basis to do direct-mail work. Noddra was owned by Willard Kauth and his wife.

The National Tuberculosis and Respiratory Disease Association[2] has been taking in over $40 million annually from American contributors. The first page of the organization's 1970–71 annual report reveals the secret of its fund-raising success: *"TUBERCULOSIS. There were 37,137 new cases of tuberculosis in 1970. . . . Direct and indirect costs of TB are one billion dollars annually."* And so on. Actually, tuberculosis is a very low-incidence disease nowadays, and as a cause of death it is almost a nonentity, ranking below hernias, ulcers, and seventeen other causes. In 1972, the Tuberculosis Association's District of Columbia chapter launched a $10,000 project designed to show how truly widespread and frightening its disease actually is. The project was directed at Washington's worst slum area, where TB was supposed to be reaching epidemic proportions. The idea was to go door to door, conducting TB tests. Of 1,129 people tested, 158 showed signs of tuberculosis. Of those 158 people, 87 reported for more ex-

[2] Shortly before publication, the organization changed its name to the "American Lung Association."

tensive testing. Further examination revealed that none of them had tuberculosis. After these astounding results were computed, the National Tuberculosis and Respiratory Disease Association declared the tests "ineffective." It is entirely possible that this declaration was made in the sincere belief that the tests were unreliable. Then again, the major problem with the tests may have been that they conflicted with the organization's fund-raising literature.

The possibility of exaggerated claims in fund-raising campaigns is certainly not the exclusive province of one charitable organization. To the contrary, the general tolerance level of deceit in charitable fund raising is remarkably low. A reasonable argument could be made that outlandish fund-raising claims actually work to reduce fund-raising costs. Just by changing a few words around, you can make your cause seem much more worthy and thereby attract more money at no additional cost. But that is really beside the point. We are dealing with charities; remember? In these times of business frauds and Watergate atrocities, our charitable organizations certainly bear some responsibility for maintaining our faith in the value of principle. And yet, when it comes to fund raising, principle has too often taken a back seat to other considerations. In many cases, our charities will claim immunity on the ground that they were simply trying to cut fund-raising costs and raise more money for their worthy causes. But I, for one, really don't give a damn whether I am being exploited in the name of profit, national security, or lower fund-raising costs. It feels just about the same.

The matter of fund raising raises questions that we must face if we are to understand and evaluate the charitable enterprises that ask for our contributions. How far is our favorite charity willing to go to raise a buck? Does it make any effort to raise money from government, private foundations, and wealthy benefactors, or is it content to sit back and turn everything over to a paid solicitor who will launch a direct-mail blitz and hope for the best? Is there a true commitment to cutting fund-raising costs, or is that just a pose for our benefit while truth is being swept under the Public Education budget?

It would be easier, of course, to accept the Civil Service Commission magic formula and leave it at that. But it just isn't possible. We know too much already. We have seen that fund raising is too unpredictable an enterprise to be a reliable measure of a charity's worth; too complex an enterprise to be accurately reflected in simple statistics. At the most, the statistics are clues of varying worth. At the least, they are inducements to further pursue our inquiry. Whether by accident or design, some horrible truths about fund raising have seeped through American charity's glittering façade. When such deep cracks appear on so perfect a surface, it is time to find out exactly what has been happening in the basement.

6   Management: The Awful Truth

I have two stories to tell you. Both are true. Each involves one interesting person and one charitable organization. We should be able to draw several morals from the stories.

The First Story

In 1963 a New York lawyer named John Keesing incorporated an organization he hoped would fulfill a long-time dream. Keesing believed that the road to world peace lay in establishing avenues of international human interaction. He felt that if people of different nations understood each other and knew each other personally, they wouldn't go around blowing each other up. ("Hey, man, I don't give a damn what the President says, my old buddy Chang Loo lives down there." And the machine would stop.) Keesing was wise enough to know that by the time human beings reach adulthood, they have accumulated too many prejudices to mingle receptively with other peoples. His idea was to beat the prejudices to the punch by introducing children of one nation to children of another nation and letting them discover each other. He hoped that his charitable organization, the Children to Children foundation, would be able to finance a large-scale children's international exchange program.

John Keesing may have been a bit overly idealistic about our chances for world peace. But when it came to charity, he had both feet firmly planted in reality. He knew he needed a celebrity to attract donations to his cause. He looked around and came up with Jeane Dixon, the Washington prophetess whose predicted assassination of President John Kennedy had just become reality, skyrocketing Dixon to international renown. Dixon accepted Keesing's offer and became president of Children to Children. Almost immediately, they entered into a bitter dispute that would last for years. Keesing wanted the organization to serve only his envisioned children's exchange program. But Jeane Dixon also had a vision: a children's medical center that would be built in Washington and named after Jeane Dixon. She demanded that Children to Children dedicate itself to that purpose.

The dispute ended when Keesing died. "Before then, Jeane Dixon was just president of Children to Children," a foundation employee told me. "After that, she *was* Children to Children." Her first act in that capacity was using foundation contributions to commission an architect's ren-

dering of the Jeane Dixon Medical Center. The rendering
shows a vast, eight-building complex with a chapel at the
center. Soaring skyward from the chapel roof, there is an
enormous spire that is topped by an eternal flame. Dixon
reproduced the rendering in a Children to Children newsletter, announced that the medical center was just around
the corner, and asked for contributions from her substantial
and devoted following. The money started coming in. Dixon
hired a small staff to administer her organization. And
then the trouble started.

One source of difficulty was the medical center itself.
Hospital experts from whom she tried to enlist support
were simply not buying it. One told me that her concept
was terribly naïve and misguided. "I sat there listening to
her and, after a while, I started getting suspicious," he
said. "So I asked her whether she was getting any advice
from medical professionals. And she said: 'Yes, from a
doctor in Switzerland.'" Others in the field told me that
the last thing Washington needed was a new hospital,
that the accepted plan for the area was to work with
existing facilities and expand them intelligently and carefully. They said that if Dixon's plans ever reached fruition,
they would cause immeasurable damage to such development. But those who had worked closely with Children to
Children were convinced that the health professionals had
no reason to lose a minute's sleep.

Former employees of the organization told me that under
Jeane Dixon's directorship the organization had been wallowing in chaos. Incoming mail was seldom opened, just
thrown into boxes which were then stacked in the basement of the Dixon real estate company. Checks from contributors were left strewn on desk tops and not deposited
for weeks. Some checks remained in the unopened mail
that was banished to the basement. Employees were re-

cruited personally by Dixon (all the Dixon employees I interviewed are now former employees). Usually they were people she met, took a liking to, and impulsively handed a job offer. Several told me that they had been lured away from good jobs with grand promises of helping mankind and salaries they could not refuse. But once in the employ of Children to Children, many found the promises unrealizable and the salaries small compensation for the anguish and frustration they encountered.

"It was a mess," one told me. "I was never sure whether I was supposed to be working for the charity, the real estate company, or Mrs. Dixon personally. I usually found myself working for all three. But the charity paid my salary." Another said: "I tried to put some order into the chaos. I really tried. But there was no way it could have been done. No way at all."

In peak years, Children to Children was taking in well over $100,000 and spending only a minute portion of its donations on a charitable purpose. In 1969, for example, it received $120,000 and spent a total of $15,000 on "Miscellaneous Child Care" and "Miscellaneous Child Education," the rest on administration. One of the organization's "child" recipients was Robert Dupré, a thirty-four-year-old opera singer who received between three thousand and five thousand dollars annually from the charity for singing lessons.

An inordinate amount of staff time was spent, not in furtherance of fund raising or improving administration, but in the service of Jeane Dixon. Some employees recalled working on Dixon's book galleys, newspaper columns, and fan mail. Others showed me copies of Children to Children newsletters, pointing out that a large part of these publications was devoted to advertising Jeane Dixon and plugging her books. One newsletter even included an order form for her latest book. Employees said that the orders were received by Children to Children staff, the books mailed out in Children to Children envelopes that had been stamped on the Children to Children postage machine. The royalties earned by Jeane Dixon on these books were paid not to the charity but to a corporation owned by Dixon and her husband.

"She doesn't look on Children to Children as a charity," one former employee told me. "If you read her latest book you'll see she predicts that we'll have a woman President by 1980. I don't have to tell you who she's thinking about. She's running for office now and she's using Children to Children as her campaign organization." Whether or not this conjecture was accurate, it does seem clear that Jeane Dixon was the major cause of the organization's difficulties.

According to her official biography, Dixon was born of well-to-do German immigrants shortly after the end of World War I; swept off her feet by James Dixon, a dashing Hollywood businessman, and married at a young age. They moved to Washington during the early 1940s and Jeane Dixon gained moderate prominence in Washington society by fortunetelling political futures with moderate accuracy. On the surface, she was a genteel aristocrat, a devout Catholic, and a magnanimous benefactress. But she was very tough as well. During the postwar land boom, the Dixons began building a thriving real estate business in Washington, and Jeane Dixon quickly acquired the reputation of being shrewd in business and unyielding in negotiations. Several Children to Children employees told me that it went even further.

"She could turn against you at the drop of a hat," one said. "And once she did, watch out! I've never known a more vindictive person. She could make up the most incredible stories about you, accuse you of the most terrible things. Usually, it was because of something that was her fault. She just couldn't take the blame for anything. It had to be someone else."

Several other people who worked with Children to Children also mentioned Dixon's reflexive tendency to blame others for her problems. There is evidence that supports this contention. The files of federal district court in Washington reveal that Jeane Dixon has been thrice sued for breach of contract since 1967. In the first suit, she counterclaimed for $70,000 in damages, accusing the plaintiff of failure to meet the contractual deadline. In the second suit, she also counterclaimed, accusing the plaintiff of stealing seven hundred dollars worth of tools. In the third suit, she also counterclaimed, accusing the plaintiff of acts "designed to harass, intimidate and harm" her and alleging that she had become physically ill as a result.

The third case involved a ghostwritten manuscript that Dixon had commissioned. She approved the completed manuscript then changed her mind and wrote a letter of rejection to her publisher. In order to explain why she had approved a manuscript she did not like, she stated, in effect, that she had been under the influence of a drug at the time. The letter reads, in part: "As you know, on Friday I was given a shot of Novocaine by Dr. ——— because of the terrible pain in my arm. Although I explained to her that Novocaine is a drug which affects my central nervous system in a most debilitating way, she insisted on giving it to me." In a subsequent deposition, she was asked about the Novocaine incident:

Q. Were you affected from the reaction of the Novocaine?

A. I do not know what you mean.

Q. In any way, shape or form?

A. No, I have no allergies. I only have allergies to cigarette smoke.

When I asked Dixon about some of the more questionable aspects of Children to Children, she blamed it on her employees, whom she accused of theft, treachery, and incompetence. She said that Martha Rountree, formerly of NBC's "Meet the Press," had been paid over seventeen thousand dollars in consultant fees by Children to Children to set up an effective direct-mail campaign and that Rountree had done "absolutely nothing" to earn it. "She didn't bring in one name, not one dollar, so help me God!"[1] Dixon went on to say that whatever I had heard from her past and present employees was a pack of lies and that if I decided to publish it, she would sue me for a million dollars.[2]

The Second Story

In 1938 Basil O'Connor was a wealthy Wall Street lawyer, a close friend and former law partner of President

[1] Of course, I have no way of verifying Dixon's allegations in this regard.

[2] This statement was made in regard to an article that was published in the April 1970 issue of the *Washingtonian Magazine*. Although Mrs. Dixon took no legal action as a result of that article, she did file suit against me for writing a second article about her three years later in the Washington *Post*. Her petition was filed in an Oklahoma state court. The petition alleged that several things I had written about Mrs. Dixon were "intentionally defamatory, knowingly false, and published in reckless disregard for the truth." These included statements that Children to Children had been founded by John Keesing rather than by Dixon; that Keesing and Dixon had a dispute over the purpose of the charity; that boxes of unopened mail were stacked in the basement and contributions left on desk tops; that Children to Children financial statements showed only 12 per cent of donations going to help children; that Children to Children newsletters advertised Dixon's books; that Martha Rountree received seventeen thousand dollars from Children to Children; and that Mrs. Dixon told me Rountree did "absolutely nothing" for the charity. The petition further alleged that Dixon had suffered one million dollars in damages as a result of the article and asked the court to award six million dollars in punitive damages as well. The suit against me was subsequently dismissed for lack of jurisdiction.

Franklin Roosevelt, and a part-time charity executive, serving as treasurer of Roosevelt's Warm Springs Foundation, which supported a small polio hospital in Georgia. Because he was himself stricken with the disease, Roosevelt had made polio his personal cause, and in 1938, it was he who announced the establishment of the National Foundation for Infantile Paralysis (later shortened by lopping off the last three words) and it was his friend Basil O'Connor who became president of the anti-polio organization. Roosevelt's deep interest in the polio fight and his affection for O'Connor were public knowledge. The Foundation's board of trustees was composed of Roosevelt's political and personal friends and of business people who were continually courting presidential favor. They gave O'Connor absolute license to run the organization as he saw fit.

He was a dapper man of expensive tastes. He had risen from the depths of poverty and, now that he had money, he was not the sort to sit and count it. He lived the good life. At the same time, he was not a frivolous person. Frivolous people do not ordinarily climb to the top of a Wall Street law firm. That kind of success requires a determined mind, a deep understanding of people, and above all, an awareness of what a successful law practice is about. Only a part of it is about law. You can always hire a bright young person to do your legal research. But attracting and maintaining enough of the right kind of clients is something else again. Most of it has to do with appearances, both in and out of court. The clothes your witness wears can frequently have a deep impact on a jury verdict. The type of car you drive, the thickness of your office carpet, the poses you assume while interviewing a client, will all have a very direct bearing on the amount and kind of business you do, and on how much you can charge to do it.

When it came to appearances, Basil O'Connor was undoubtedly a genius. After assuming command of the National Foundation, he changed the nature of American charity almost overnight, sculpturing that glittering façade we know today. In 1938, his first act as president of the new organization was launching a fund-raising campaign unlike anything the nation had seen. Eddie Cantor, Jack Benny, and even the Lone Ranger took to the airwaves in a massive media blitz on behalf of the polio fight.

O'Connor's techniques involved much more than celebrities. He disdained the usual appeal to public conscience and good citizenry. Instead, he went right for the gut. He hauled out the crippled children and paraded them before the parents of other children. "There but for the grace of God," he told them, over and over, in countless different ways. In the fund-raising literature O'Connor masterminded, polio was never just a disease. It was an "epidemic," sometimes even a "pestilence." It was always widespread and terrible.

The American public responded to these fund-raising techniques with compassion, with panic, and with an enormous amount of money. That first campaign, in 1938, attracted over $1.8 million in contributions, a monumental achievement in that time and place. From then on, the money just poured in, averaging nearly $30 million annually during the following twenty years. In the end, the American public got what it wanted from the National Foundation: the outright conquest of polio. The lion's share of credit for the Salk vaccine must be given to O'Connor and his organization. Salk's research and the related work of his fellow scientists were in large part financed by Foundation money. The National Foundation also arranged for and financed production and distribution of much of the vaccine.

It was an extraordinary achievement by any standard.

On the other hand, the National Foundation attracted and spent nearly $550 million of other people's money between 1938 and 1958. In several respects, the manner in which these funds were raised and managed is less than commendable.

Basil O'Connor's fund-raising method was the object of loud and repeated criticism from health and charity professionals. Many doctors believed that O'Connor had created an unwarranted panic reaction to polio in this country, causing parents to rush their children to the hospital at the first sign of a sore muscle. The charity people objected to O'Connor's panic-building because they believed it resulted in too much money pouring into National Foundation coffers, to the disadvantage of charities dealing with other health problems that were at least equally serious. Contrary to National Foundation fund-raising claims, polio was actually a rather low-incidence disease in this country, averaging less than thirty thousand new cases nationwide during the twenty-year anti-polio drive, with less than twenty thousand cases in many "epidemic" years. Moreover, contrary to the National Foundation's crippled-child image, only about half of polio cases were paralytic in nature and many victims were adults.

The Foundation's "fight polio" pitch led many contributors to believe that all or most of their money would be used for research. Actually, only about 6 per cent of that $550 million was spent for this purpose. Trying to determine how the rest of the money was spent is a frustrating undertaking. National Foundation annual reports from this period are remarkably uninformative. For several years, the organization did not even bother to report on the half of its receipts that was given to chapters. When it began accounting for chapter expenditures, this was based on treasurers' reports, not on audits. In reporting expenditures by national headquarters, the Foundation used broad and uninformative expenditure categories such as "epidemic aid" and "polio prevention," and terribly confusing accounting techniques. Through it all, Basil O'Connor made no attempt to hide his lack of commitment to meaningful disclosure of his organization's financial activities.

Despite all this, there was sufficient information on O'Connor's activities to gain him the reputation of being one of the most spendthrift executives in American charity. For example, in 1951 and 1952 O'Connor spent nearly $500,000 of Foundation funds to test a gamma-globulin component which was thought to offer protection against polio. The tests showed that gamma globulin provided very limited and very temporary protection at best. Nevertheless, in 1953 O'Connor spent $5 million to buy up every drop of gamma globulin in the country. In the same year, he issued a grant to Armour Laboratories for the purchase of a $500,000 machine that could produce gamma globulin. And in 1954, when the Salk vaccine was already in production, O'Connor purchased another $9 million worth of gamma globulin.

One of O'Connor's most questionable arrangements was serving as president of both the National Foundation and the Georgia Warm Springs Foundation—Roosevelt's small polio hospital and a National Foundation grantee. Between 1938 and 1958, the Georgia hospital received over $5 million in grants from National Foundation headquarters. It also received more than $10 million from National Foundation chapters. There are several reasons to question the entitlement of Warm Springs to these staggering sums. For one thing, it was a distinctly regional institution, the great majority of its patients coming from the South, particularly from Georgia. It was not a very large facility, having a 100-bed capacity through most of its existence. Many of the patients it treated paid their own way and, in some years, Warm Springs received several hundred thousand dollars in private donations. It is not unreasonable to conclude that the major reason O'Connor's National Foundation was so nice to this facility was that O'Connor was its president.

There is more. In 1956, O'Connor spent $500,000 to finance a study that would determine what the National Foundation should do after polio. The 1958 annual report reveals that a total of $8.1 million was spent on "epidemic aid." There were less than six thousand polio cases reported that year, only a fraction of them serious. What epidemic? O'Connor himself was living on a National Foundation expense account, the amount of which was considered the organization's deepest secret. Judging by O'Connor's fancy tastes and Waldorf Astoria suite, however, his expenses could not have been inconsequential.

Basil O'Connor died shortly before I began researching this book. We must therefore settle for secondhand reports of his views. In *The Gentle Legions* (Doubleday, 1961), Richard Carter reports asking O'Connor about his alleged spendthriftiness, and he quotes O'Connor's reply: "Why do you suppose the people gave us the money? They wanted us to fight polio. So we fought polio."

These two stories have several themes in common. Each discusses a charitable organization that spent its contributions on some questionable purposes. There were fundraising abuses in both cases, but these were merely symptoms of much more serious problems. And in each case, the problems seem to have been attributable in great part to the person running the organization. Yes, there are people back there—real, human, flesh-and-blood people—spending our charitable contributions. It seems obvious. But think about it for a moment. Does that thought occur to you when you make a donation? Of course not. If you can manage to get past the crippled child or the dreaded disease, you run up against an inanimate slogan or symbol, and perhaps as far as the inanimate organization it represents— but seldom through all the layers to the people who spend your money. Yet, between 1938 and 1958, one person was given $550 million of other people's money to spend as he wished. Why Basil OConnor? How did he and Jeane Dixon ascend to their public trusteeships?

Most of us don't have the time, energy, or interest to go around recruiting people for our favorite cause and leading them to victory. Those who engage in such activities must first have the time to take on low-paying or no-paying assignments, which usually means that they are wealthy to begin with. They must also have a strong motivation to leave the comfort of their homes. This can range from the compassion of a Clara Barton and the outrage of a Jane Addams to such less noble inspirations as power seeking, image building, and outright greed. By force of these circumstances, there are not very many people available to assume leadership roles. And we can further eliminate those who cannot attract the right kind of support for their candidacies because they lack one of the three c's: clout, charisma, and connections.

The most obvious problem arising from this process of natural selection is the elimination of all but one viewpoint and one experience from the people who dictate our destiny. But an equally serious and less apparent difficulty comes from our tendency to muddle the distinction between a leader and an administrator. It happens all the time in the political world. Winning an election and running a government require two very different sets of human abilities. But both jobs go to the same person. The same is true in the charity world. Clara Barton was a giant when it came to charismatic leadership, but she was a terrible administrator, and her inability to account for Red Cross funds caused a scandal that nearly doomed the organization in its infancy. Her only qualification for the administrative job was that she had founded the organization; it was "her baby." Jeane Dixon and Basil O'Connor were each selected to launch a new organization—which means such things as fund raising, publicity, and image building. In each case, a reasonable argument can be made to support the choice for that kind of assignment. And even though running an organization is a different matter entirely, they acquired that job as well, like Barton, Flick, and so many others before them.

Where did they fall short? A partial answer, in symbolic form, is provided by Jeane Dixon herself. In *A Gift of Prophecy* (Morrow, 1965), Ruth Montgomery quotes Dixon's description of a vision she experienced at 3:14 A.M. on July 14, 1952, while she was lying in bed:

> Suddenly, I could feel a physical motion against the mattress, to the left side of my head. I rolled onto my left side, facing the east, and as I did so I saw the body of a snake. It was no bigger around than a garden hose, and I could see neither its head nor its tail. I felt its powerful little body twisting down the side of my bed and raising the corner of the mattress at the foot. Then, though I seemed cloaked in a substance as soft as eiderdown, I could feel its head nudging beneath my ankles, and its body growing larger as it wrapped itself around my legs and hips. I was not frightened. I knew instinctively that I was to be shown how little I knew about life. As the snake gradually entwined itself around my chest I could see its head

but not its eyes. They were gazing towards the east, rather than at me. By this time the snake was as big around as a man's arm. . . . It turned its head, looking to the east and then at me, as if to say that I too must look to the east for God's wisdom and guidance. . . . I knew that I had God's protection, for the steady gaze of the reptile was permeated with love, goodness, strength and knowledge. A sense of "peace on earth, good will toward men" coursed through my being.

Leaving the Freudians to their field day, let us consider an even more curious aspect of this Dixon vision with a historical note on her early-morning visitor: *And the Lord God said unto the serpent: "Because thou hast done this, cursed art thou from among all cattle, and from among all beasts of the field; upon thy belly thou shalt go, and dust shalt thou eat all the days of thy life.* Genesis 3:14.[3] And ever since, the serpent has been universally considered Satan's tool. It certainly seems strange that God should have selected such a creature to deliver a message to Jeane Dixon. But wait! In *My Life and Prophecies* (Morrow, 1969), written for Jeane Dixon by Rene Noorbergen, there is a new description of the Dixon snake vision. The lurid details are gone—no more nudging beneath ankles or entwining around legs, hips, and chest. And in the end, there is a simple Dixon quote: "Satan showed himself to me as a serpent." Dixon was asked about this discrepancy in a subsequent court deposition:

Q. Going back to the serpent for a minute, did the serpent appear as the Devil or as the messenger of God?
A. My book will tell you that.

[3] Symbolism freaks should note that the chapter-and-verse number is exactly the same as the time of the Dixon vision.

Q. I am asking you. You are under oath.

A. The serpent as it came to me was bringing a message for the people of the world.

Q. Was it bringing a message from the Devil or from God?

A. From the Lord. The Devil doesn't bring me messages.

(Which leaves Jeane Dixon's followers in pretty much of a dither as to whether to look east or west for God's wisdom.)

This effectively disproves the common belief that it is an easy matter to distinguish God from Satan. It certainly is not. And yet, in her two public roles—visionary and charity executive—this is exactly what Jeane Dixon was obligated to do: for the sake of all the people who had invested their faith and hard-earned cash in her books, in her charity, and in Jeane Dixon personally. Her problems with the serpent are mainly attributable to the fact that visions are vulnerable to the prejudices of the human mind and the demands of the human ego. Similar forces are at work in the charity world.

In trying to distinguish right from wrong in their roles as charity executives, Jeane Dixon and Basil O'Connor were functioning with their personal experiences of years in the business world. In business, money is obtained from people who can arm themselves with the latest issue of *Consumer Reports* and who are protected by the Uniform Commercial Code. Not so in the charity world. In business, a 10 per cent net profit is considered perfectly reasonable. Not so for a charity fund-raising drive. These and many other attitudes from the marketplace simply have no place in a well-run and publicly oriented charitable organization. But there is substantial evidence that they throve during the O'Connor and the Dixon administrations. And there is that ancient tool of Satan—temptation.

The major initial consequence of the American public's

massive investment in the polio fight was not a cure for
polio. Rather, it was the erection of a gigantic bureaucracy
where no organization had existed. At the head of that
bureaucracy and in absolute control was a single individual
named O'Connor. For three decades, it was his private
kingdom. No matter how great his success on Wall Street,
no law firm on earth could have offered him the fringe
benefits provided by the National Foundation. He had at
his command three million volunteers and one of the largest
professional staffs in the charity world. At the snap of his
fingers, he could obtain a newspaper headline for himself.
Children to Children offered similar benefits to Jeane Dixon,
though on a much smaller scale, of course. Through the
organization, she acquired a staff she did not have to pay,
a newsletter to boost her image, and a charitable cause to
call her own. When a human being has that much ego invested in an enterprise, the temptations are numerous and
very real. There is no way you can eternally engrave the
name "Jeane Dixon" on a children's exchange program.
There may have been more worthy grantees than the
Georgia Warm Springs Foundation, but they had nothing
to offer the prestige of Basil O'Connor. Failing to purchase
even one drop of gamma globulin would have had absolutely no effect on Salk's research. But there would have
been $14 million dollars in the National Foundation kitty
at year's end, which could have had dire consequences for
O'Connor and his organization: they would have been
forced to abandon the critical-need-for-funds approach so
essential to effective fund raising in the voluntary health
field. More important, the less an organization spends, the
less justification for a large staff to administer its budget.

These considerations are not at all limited to one organization, one individual, or even to one level of charity
management. Throughout the charity world, employees,

volunteers, consultants, and people of all shapes and responsibilities have personal biases and interests that will have a direct bearing on whether the organization views a particular alternative as God or the Devil in terms of charitable purpose. There is no way to convince a salaried employee that a pay increase would violate the organization's public duty. The same applies to the executive's expense account, the secretary's new typewriter, and the nephew's carpeted laboratory. Conscience is malleable and private, and usually much weaker than self-interest. There is one self-interest that runs through every level of charity management. Even if you are associated with a perfect charity—an organization that has a valid cause, reasonable fund-raising methods and costs, efficient management, and enough money to spend on its programs—you will still be unhappy if you mention the name of your organization at the singles bar and receive only a blank stare in return. You want them to bow in respect at the sound of your organization's name. You want them to introduce you as spokesperson for the "esteemed" charitable organization.

In the charity world, esteem is obtainable, not only through accomplishment but also through wealth, bigness, and renown. In fact, accomplishment in certain charitable areas is, by force of circumstance, a very rare commodity indeed. It took seventeen years and two hundred fifty times what the respected Damon Runyon-Walter Winchell Cancer Fund spends annually on cancer research to find a cure for polio. Sixty years after the American Cancer Society was founded, there is still no cure for cancer.

There is, of course really no way to tell exactly how much a particular organization unnecessarily invests in its own esteem. A research grant is reported as a research grant even if the organization is interested only in purchasing the scientist's reputation and the scientist is interested only in resting on a Nobel prize. We cannot spend a week in the new employee's office to determine whether that person is really needed by the organization or is just another brick in the executive director's expanding empire. Nevertheless, we must not close our eyes to the fact that American charity has more than its share of empires.

Take the voluntary health field, for example. In 1971, $360 million was spent by some thirty health charities. Five of those organizations—the American Cancer Society, the American Heart Association, the National Easter Seal Society, the National Tuberculosis and Respiratory Disease Association, and the National Foundation—spent a combined total of $241 million, nearly 70 per cent of the total voluntary health expenditure. A second tier, of four organizations, spent 16 per cent of the total, leaving less than 15 per cent of the charity health budget to 70 per cent of our health charities. We could take the easy way and accept Basil O'Connor's view: those nine monstrous charities became monstrous because the public "wanted" them to have most of the charity dollar. But this ignores the fact that O'Connor spent many millions of dollars to make the public want to fight polio. Or we could say that each organization developed according to public need; the bigger the organization the greater the need for it. But how? Those charities certainly did not arise and expand of their own accord. There were, and still are, people back there, forming the policy, drawing the design, and working with the bricks and mortar. Whatever the reasons for their participation, I can conceive of no motive that would cause them to object to their organization becoming the largest and most powerful charity the market would allow.

One of the most troublesome aspects of the voluntary health statistics is that two of the big five organizations were established to fight polio and tuberculosis, diseases for which cures and immunizations are now very much available. Rather than disbanding, the National Foundation changed its cause to fighting birth defects and the tuberculosis group added "respiratory disease" to its name. Together, they account for $70 million of annual health-charity expenditures. Why didn't they go out of business when they successfully conquered the diseases they set out to fight? The organizations say there was a public need and a public desire for them to enter new fields. But what about the executives who would have been out of work, the scientists who would have been forced to shop elsewhere for their research grants, the board members who would have had no charity to place beside their names in Who's Who?

The prophylactic against unnecessary empire building, empire nurturing, and executive nest feathering is supposed to be the organization's board of trustees (or directors), an impartial body of good citizens who receive no compensation for their services. The most obvious difficulty with such a watchdog group is that the trustees themselves maintain a strong interest in elevating their organization above all others in power and esteem. They are not the most likely people to vote in favor of closing up shop or against adding another employee to the Public Education Division. But they are the most likely people to ask why there was no prenatal-care booklet in their doctor's office, publicizing the organization. Furthermore, even the most conscientious board member is hampered by a limited involvement in the organization. The board member buzzes into town once in a while, looks around, attends a couple of meetings, and is gone. The executives and their paid staff remain. Moreover, the executives—if not selected by the board in the first place—were certainly approved by the trustees, at least partially on the basis of personal qualities. In an amiable relationship, there is a great tendency to give the benefit of the doubt.

It took the trustees of the Sister Kenny Insitute over ten years to learn that Kline and Koolish were robbing the organization blind. It took an SEC investigation and a lawsuit to teach trustees of the Jesuit Fathers of Houston that Frank Sharp's shady activities had cost their organization over $6 million and driven it to the edge of bankruptcy. How many charity executives and charity promoters are now filling their pockets under the noses of equally unobservant watchdogs? There is no way to tell. We only see the truly outrageous scandals that are pulled to the surface, usually through the efforts of outside investigators. One of them, still in the headlines at the time of this writing, involves the United Service Organizations (USO), sponsor of all those Bob Hope Viet Nam tours and of USO military clubs around the world. The association's board of governors reads like the social register and includes some of the most astute business people in the nation. Nevertheless, between 1965 and 1970, USO employees in Viet Nam used USO facilities and bank accounts for profitable black marketeering, at an estimated cost to the USO in excess of $5 million.

In a complicated scheme, USO executives would forge purchase slips for merchandise that their clubs never ordered and never received. They would then draw USO funds to cover the fake purchase orders and keep the money themselves or send it on to a bank in Switzerland. There were more complicated refinements involving the exchange of military and Vietnamese money for U.S. dollars —at a profit, of course, and at the expense of the USO. If the board of governors discovered what was going on, there was no sign of it. Samuel Anderson, head of Viet Nam operations at the height of the profiteering, was promoted to executive director of the USO.

In April 1972, Congressman Les Aspin (D., Wisconsin) introduced into the Congressional Record considerable evidence of the USO black-market activity, including statements by former USO employees. Anderson denied that he was involved, and the USO board of governors refused to fire him. One board member referred to this decision as "courageous." In January 1973, Anderson submitted his resignation, which was accepted. It is entirely possible that Samuel Anderson was free of guilt and resigned only to save the USO further embarrassment. But we cannot accept that possibility without at least considering the equally likely notion that the board knew what was happening all along or that it believed Anderson was at least partially responsible and remained silent in order to save the USO further embarrassment.

In the charity business we are usually forced to settle for equal possibilities. Officials of the United States Olympic Committee tell us that it was absolutely necessary for 146 non-athletes to travel to Munich at our expense to take care of 400 athletes. Perhaps there is also a reasonable explanation for the fact that none of those 146 people prevented the banning of Bob Seagren's fiber-glass pole, or even lodged an official protest: or for the fact that the job of getting U.S. sprinters to the track on time was given to one unmonitored person, a person easily confused by time schedules. At the same time, there is another possible explanation for all these occurrences: that the people running the Olympic organization were using our money to have one hell of a good time in Munich.

We are neither prosecutors nor judges. It is not for us to weigh every shred of evidence or to build irrefutable cases. In considering that massive charity enterprise, the possibilities alone are enough. We are only poor, disconnected contributors. All we want is some reasonable assurance that at least most of our money is going for a decent and useful purpose. We have certainly been given that kind of assurance by the charity people—over and over, through myths and slogans and Madison Avenue imagery. But there is an awful truth lurking in the shadows of the charity world. It is simply that the assurance does not exist. We cannot trust the lofty-sounding name. It may be a cover for a charity profiteer. We cannot trust protective laws and agencies. They do not exist. We cannot trust simplistic formulas that can be applied to superficial statistics. The formulas do not work and the statistics may be misleading— which leaves us with a lot of equal possibilities all around.

A particular fund-raising percentage may be perfectly reasonable or absolutely outrageous. A charitable cause may fill a valid social need or reflect the egotistical whimsies of the people who control the organization. The size of a particular organization may be the result of careful and reasonable planning or of power seeking by executives and board members. Once we cut away the myths and approach charity in the same way we approach any other human endeavor in this nation, we can expect to find that American charity, like the American Football Conference, will have a few organizations at each end of the spectrum and a lot of organizations in the middle.

To be sure, charity is a world like none other, with its own peculiar characteristics, vested interests, operating variables, and unpredictabilities. But, then, so is football. In both cases, the most unpredictable variable of all is the human one, which makes forecasting the outcome of a game or a charity dollar considerably less than certain. But in the football world, people such as Jimmy the Greek do it all the time with remarkable accuracy by studying a team's personnel and its performance record. It seems a sensible thing to try in the charity world as well.

Part 3

The Charity Organization

7   The First Charity

The few blocks of Seventeenth Street that run past the White House contain a series of imposing structures from the architectural past, each a monument to tradition. Various phases of American life and thought are represented: culture, finance, patriotism, government. And alongside these, nearly abutting the Daughters of the American Revolution and a mere stone's throw from our presidential palace itself, American charity has been given a most appropriate recognition.

It is a gleaming white building of many pillars. Marble

busts of Faith, Hope, and Charity adorn its corridors. On stained-glass windows and garden statuary, angels of mercy forever tend the sick and wounded. During working hours, a large black limousine, license tag "ANRC," stands in silent majesty, tires firmly planted on the circular driveway. And above the Grecian entrance, there is the symbol that says it all: a red cross. Nothing else would do. The American (National) Red Cross is the oldest charitable organization in the nation. It is also the largest, in both money and manpower. No other charity can hope to match the renown of its name or the prestige of its officers. The President of the United States is its honorary chairman. The Attorney General and the Secretary of the Treasury serve as honorary counselor and honorary treasurer, respectively. And at fund-raising time, the cream of Hollywood and Madison Avenue, corporate executives, Washington politicians, and military brass join in a mad rush for the Red Cross bandwagon.

It is an awesome enterprise: a bureaucracy of massive proportions, an object of idol worship for nearly two million blindly loyal volunteers, and an institution that has engraved itself upon the face of American history with remarkable regularity. At the same time, the Red Cross has been in the eye of controversy since its infancy—a target of angry criticism and a source of considerable misunderstanding.

A major cause of misconception is the fact that two types of organizations bear the Red Cross name. The International Committee of the Red Cross, headquartered in Geneva, is an all-Swiss organization founded by Henri Dunant in 1863. It is dedicated to the promotion of humanitarian international law, primarily through the Geneva Conventions. The American National Red Cross, founded by Clara Barton in 1881, is one of numerous Red Cross

societies around the world—national organizations which
were inspired by Dunant's International Committee and
which support the work of the Swiss groups. The national
societies were initially founded for the sole purpose of serving as civilian hospital corps for their armies. They later
expanded their mission to include hospital service in times
of natural disaster. The national societies belong to their
own international conference, which is mostly a mutual-
friendship association. It has no formal connection to the
International Committee.

The American Red Cross is the largest of the national
societies. This fact alone has given birth to some criticism
at the international level by Red Cross societies in smaller
nations, which look to big brother for assistance in times
of trouble and find it lacking or insufficient. While such
great expectations are understandable, they overlook the
fact that our Red Cross society bears a proportionately
larger charitable burden on its home soil than that of the
smaller societies that serve much smaller populations and
have undertaken fewer responsibilities.

Similar forces are at work on a national level. During
World War II, while looser wartime sexual morals were
smiled upon by all, both here and abroad, the Red Cross
found itself the target of vicious attacks because its women
volunteers did not carry chastity belts with them to overseas duty. British Red Cross chapters charged their military
people small fees for meals and lodging. There was not a
whimper. When the American Red Cross units in Britain
did the same, there was a scandal. In these and other
instances, we demanded more than the Red Cross could
deliver, perhaps more than the Red Cross should have delivered, and we turned against the organization for failing
to fulfill our expectations.

At the same time, these expectations were thrust upon us

through decades of Red Cross image building, traceable to Clara Barton herself. In order to gain funds and recognition for her cause and its handful of supporters, Barton was forced to battle the apathy of average Americans and the outright disdain of the elite toward the do-gooders of the charity world. The weapons she chose are succinctly described, in Charles Hurd's *The Compact History of the American Red Cross* (Hawthorn, 1959), by one chapter title: "Publicity, Propaganda and Politics." Barton dramatized the activities of her charity as often as possible. She courted the dignitaries at every opportunity. She continually sought out newspaper reporters and photographers. Her poses for the camera were always dramatic, her dress usually bedecked with medals. Barton would certainly have risen to the top of Madison Avenue if she were alive today. Indeed, the seeds she planted nearly a century ago have blossomed into a major Red Cross public-relations enterprise.

There is no telling how much Red Cross time and money are invested in public relations. In 1970, the last year the organization identified such costs on its annual report, they amounted to $3.6 million. According to comptroller James Illig, this figure included salaries of people officially assigned to public-relations work, and the cost of the materials they used. It did not include the salaries of employees in other areas who may have devoted some of their time to image building. There are indications that the organization's investment in such activity is rather substantial, extending far beyond its public-relations office.

A Red Cross staff manual, distributed to more than two thousand field representatives, states: "Your public relations 'career' started the day you joined the Red Cross staff. As a full-time PR man, you have the responsibility of creating favorable attitudes among personnel at your station

toward the Red Cross." The manual provides specific in-
structions in image-building techniques: "Show the Red
Cross emblem in every photo (but do so as subtly as
possible)." And then: "Try to choose the most vivacious,
photogenic volunteers in the group as your leading ladies.
Pick clean-cut attractive patients to feature in the photos.
Remember that by carefully choosing your subjects, you
are helping to create a positive and favorable public image
of the Red Cross volunteer." The manual goes on to provide
detailed suggestions for promotional displays: "Photo No. 4
shows close-up of friendly, vivacious volunteer pointing
out objects in a museum showcase to interested patient.
Photo No. 5 shows volunteer leading patients in community
singing aboard bus returning them to their hospital. Photo
No. 6 shows patients giving volunteers grateful thanks as
they enter hospital portals."

It seems harmless enough at first glance. But multiply it
by two thousand, add ten thousand chapter employees, and
crank in the ninety years or so since Barton started the ball
rolling. The total comes out to a lot of time, money, and
energy devoted to idealizing the American Red Cross. And
when you deal in such extreme images, you force your
supporting public to respond in an extreme fashion: you are
either beloved for what you really are not or despised
because of what you cannot be. Neither alternative is very
palatable for an organization that intends to stay in business
for a while and meet the charitable challenges of a real and
very unideal world.

The Red Cross public-relations office in Washington is
less of a glossy-photograph enterprise than a communications service. The staff is composed mostly of no-nonsense
professionals who turn out press releases, help write Red
Cross literature, and advise other staff people on media
matters. They have done a considerable amount of good for

the Red Cross and the public. Edwin Powers, a member of the public-relations staff, told me: "When I first came here, most of them thought that public relations meant running away from anyone who wanted information. Our biggest triumph was getting them to sit down with someone like you and lay it all out." Indeed, with Powers leading the way, I found all the doors open and, more often than not, candid replies to my questions.

On the other hand, the sign on the door clearly labels Edwin Powers and his associates as public-relations people, not journalists. Those hired to do public-relations work are advocates, and the job of an advocate is to emphasize the strengths of his or her position, not its weaknesses. A natural consequence of nearly every public-relations enterprise is, therefore, some misleading of the public.

While researching this book, I asked just about everyone I met a single question: "On which of its programs do you think the Red Cross spends most of its money and staff time?" The answer was "disaster relief" from about 90 per cent of the people I questioned, the rest splitting between water safety and the blood program. No one mentioned Red Cross services to members of the military, by far its most expensive program. Pete Upton, who heads the Red Cross public-relations staff, was not at all surprised by the results of my informal survey. "Ever since the Viet Nam War became so damned unpopular, we've given the military program a low profile," he told me. Upton also admitted that several surveys that showed disaster relief as one of the most attractive charitable causes for potential contributors may have had some influence on his emphasis of this program in Red Cross literature.

Much more distressing than the public-relations work of Upton and his staff is the fact that Red Cross image building is not restricted to Upton's office. People throughout the organization are told that they share the responsibility of making the Red Cross look good—which raises some serious questions. In 1970 the Red Cross claimed it had 2.3 million volunteers. In 1971 the figure dropped to 1.8 million. The difference was not caused by a mass flight from Red Cross service. Rather, a 1971 study disclosed that chapters had been counting a volunteer more than once if that volunteer was involved in more than one program. Was this accident or amateur public relations? And what about the chapter volunteer who provides data on the number of people enrolled in a safety course? Or the personnel officer who estimates the number of blacks and young people who are joining the Red Cross? This is not to say that Red Cross statistics should, out of hand, be ruled as flights of fancy. But there is sufficient overindulgence in image making to justify our concern. Is it truth or just another glossy photograph? When we ask the real Red Cross to stand up, we had better look very carefully.

Several things are clear: First, the American Red Cross does a considerable amount of good. It provides half the nation's blood supply. In 1971 its safety program trained over four million people, and its disaster-relief services assisted over seventy-four thousand families. Equally important, and perhaps more so, is the fact that the Red Cross is not just an alms-giving charity. It is a community-service organization with nearly two million volunteers who spend countless hours helping their less fortunate neighbors. In a way, this is a program unto itself, giving many retired persons an opportunity to lead productive and rewarding lives.

Second, and working in at least partial balance, Red Cross resources are awesome. Its annual budget is either $175 million or $134 million, depending on whether you agree with a revised accounting system for the blood program, which I do not (see below). It employs over thirteen thousand people and, of course, has almost one hundred fifty times as many volunteers. With that kind of money and manpower, even the most inefficient and misguided organization should be able to crank out some impressive statistics. Whether they are impressive enough in the case of the Red Cross is another matter.

Third, the oft-heard criticism of the Red Cross being traditionbound, lacking sufficient aggressiveness in exploring new charity needs and catering to a WASPish view of American charity, has, for the most part, been accurate and continues to be accurate today. Part of the blame must again be placed at the feet of Clara Barton.

In Barton's view, her young organization would never achieve success by bucking the establishment. It needed a Congressional charter. It needed endorsements and money from the rich and powerful. So she relentlessly courted the "right" people and, more often than not, won them over to her cause. As a result, her organization underwent a change in both composition and outlook. No longer was the Red Cross a group of daring zealots, ready to defy the status quo in the name of charity. Its members now *were* the establishment. And the more it grew, the more establishment oriented it became—not only through deliberate selection, but also through natural circumstance. The initial battle having been won, the zealots went on to new battles. The people who replaced them were those who could afford the time. And in those days, free time seldom filtered down past the elite. And so the Red Cross acquired its image: an old white woman in a starched white uniform—Lady Bountiful toting a basketful of goodies prepared by the maid.

According to Red Cross literature, the organization and its membership have undergone dramatic changes in recent times. Its 1972 annual report begins with a general discussion of Red Cross activities that is replete with such phrases as "dissolving racial and economic barriers" and "volunteers from the total spectrum of society." It is an old Red Cross refrain. When Richard Carter was writing *The Gentle Legions* during the late 1950s, he was told about the great strides being made in democratizing and disestablish-mentizing the Red Cross. The organization began its 1966 annual report with: "During the 85 years of its existence, the American Red Cross has constantly demonstrated its responsiveness to change by adapting its programs to meet new demands and by discontinuing programs when they have become outmoded." This was simply not true in 1966. It remains mostly untrue today.

In 1972 the Red Cross created a new staff position with the exclusive responsibility of evaluating existing programs and initiating new ones. Dick Bjuberg, a Red Cross career employee who was appointed to the position, says he has encountered plenty of resistance to new directions from both staff and volunteers. He admits that even the dis-appointing statistics on chapter involvement in new pro-grams—only 10 per cent of the chapters report programs on drug abuse, less than 1 per cent on juvenile delinquency —are probably overstatements, more of that Red Cross image building. The keynote speakers at the 1972 Red Cross national convention showed no dramatic departure from tradition: Julie Eisenhower, two Army generals, a vice-president of the Pepsi-Cola Company, and Sylvia Porter Collins.

Annual reports from the past decade show that Red Cross expenditures have changed in two areas: disaster relief and blood. The incredible number of natural disasters we have experienced during the past few years has sent disaster-relief costs skyrocketing. In 1972 such costs were three times as great as they were in 1967. Of course, this change was forced upon the organization and does not reflect an involvement in new charity areas. The change in blood-program expenditures is illusory. In 1971 the Red Cross simply changed its accounting method for this program. Instead of reporting blood-program costs after deducting fees received by the organization to allay those costs (an accurate reflection of true expenditures), the Red Cross now states blood fees as income and gives blood-program costs without deducting those fees. In this way, reported blood-program costs skyrocketed from about $15 million to over $50 million in a year's time. They are really still about $15 million. So, all in all, the Red Cross spends its money in pretty much the same way it did ten years ago.

On the other hand, we have certainly learned the dangers of relying on superficial statistics alone, or even on the facts that appear immediately below the surface of such statistics. When we dig down another level, we discover that, sure enough, there have been some recent changes in the organization. The most significant is George Elsey, who became president of the Red Cross in 1970. Elsey is a dollar-a-year-man type who has spent many years in high-level government service, usually under Democratic administrations. He now spends his time trying to find ways to loosen up the vast Red Cross bureaucracy. He has, in fact, nearly completed a nationwide decentralization plan that will bring supplies and staff talent closer to individual chapters. Services to the community will undoubtedly be improved as a result. George Elsey is refreshingly candid. In 1970, when the all-black National Medical Association accused the Red Cross of ignoring black communities during a Mississippi tornado, the organization's pre-Elsey reply was a vehement denial. Today Elsey admits that disaster relief during the tornado was indeed slow in some areas and he cites racial tension as one of the causes. Elsey claims he wants to eliminate such occurrences in the future, lead the Red Cross in new directions, and make the organization more responsive to community needs. To prove he means what he says, Elsey can point to changes other than his decentralization plan.

From Richard Carter's *The Gentle Legions*: "The first thing that needs to be known about the Red Cross is that it is a private organization, and stanchly so. It subsists on voluntary contributions of time, talent and funds. Except for real estate grants, it has never taken a penny from government and vows it never will." In 1971 the Red Cross entered into a $600,000 contract to conduct blood research for the federal government. In 1972 it entered into a $2 million contract with the federal government to locate elderly people entitled to welfare and teach them about the food-stamp program. Both jobs are well suited to Red Cross resources and talent. And it is certainly nice to know that the organization is loosening its views of its own purpose and no longer rejecting needed funds out of emotional fear of creeping socialism. Another refreshing change is the creation of Dick Bjuberg's new position. Before this time, there was no one on the Red Cross staff who had the exclusive responsibility of looking beneath the grand claims, judging the distance between reality and the glossy photograph, and finding ways to close the gap.

These are very real signs of hope that come from the depths of the organization. But, at the same level, there is another truth that works very much against that hope. It is the Red Cross military-services program. From 1968 through 1972 the organization spent a total of $671 million on its various programs (I am using the old method of accounting for the blood-program expenditures). During those five years, $263 million, or 38 per cent of program expenditures, went for services to members of the armed forces. In

1971 the Red Cross national career staff consisted of 3,679 people. Of these, 2,261 employees, or just over 60 per cent of the national staff, worked for the military program (the Red Cross does not have a similar breakdown for its ten thousand chapter employees; a rough estimate according to cost figures is that about 30 per cent of chapter staff time is spent on the military program).

The program includes financial assistance to service people, counseling, and recreation. The Red Cross maintains a hookup to the Defense Department communications system which enables Red Cross overseas representatives to contact local chapters and handle family problems and other matters for military personnel in Europe and Asia. It is a big and expensive job. There is no reason to doubt that, on the whole, the Red Cross is doing the job well. Whether it should be doing the job at all is something else again. The cost to the organization has certainly been astronomical, and not only in money.

Between 1945 and 1970 three of the organization's six chief executives were retired military officers, two serving in unbroken succession during the last dozen of those years. They were complemented by people of similar backgrounds who continue to serve on the Red Cross staff. Comptroller James Illig is a retired army general. Robert Lewis, who heads the military services program, speaks more like an army officer than a civilian. "You can get that way after spending most of your life on military bases," another employee told me.

Illig and Lewis seem to be very competent people. But after a long and happy life with the military, they and others like them will certainly tend to give the armed forces every concession, whether as private individuals or as Red Cross employees. Add to this the fact that the Red Cross receives over $15 million annually in supporting services from the

Defense Department—living quarters, shipping, communications, transportation—and you have the makings of a very well-oiled relationship, of Red Cross service, not to members of the military but to the military itself. Thus we find Robert Lewis recalling: "Sometimes, we don't have any choice in what we do here. Take those clubmobiles (touring recreation facilities), for example. When we started pulling them out of Viet Nam and Korea, the Pentagon raised all kinds of hell. So we left them in Korea. What could we do?"

The most extraordinary thing about this enterprise is that no other national Red Cross society in the world provides services to its armed forces in peacetime. American Red Cross officials say that this mission is made obligatory by the organization's Congressional charter. Not so. The charter, while a bit vague on the point, was issued in 1900. The Red Cross did not begin providing peacetime services to members of the military until after World War II. During the First World War, the American Red Cross swelled to gigantic proportions, attracting more volunteers than it could use and spending $400 million in two years. But after the war the organization deflated almost overnight, rising again in the 1940s to meet the challenge of wartime. In 1945 the chief executive of the Red Cross looked around and saw that the war was over and that natural disasters had hit an all-time low. The two primary missions of his organization had suddenly become mini-missions. In order to prevent what had occurred after the First World War, the head of the Red Cross simply invented a new program: service to members of the military in peacetime. The name of the chief executive? Why, Basil O'Connor, of course. O'Connor spent five years after the war doing double duty as head of both the Red Cross and the National Foundation. He also initiated the Red Cross blood program, for which we certainly owe him our gratitude.

"Don't judge us by what we were, judge us by what we are today," Red Cross employees tell me, over and over. But if we take a good look at today, we see an organization that may be trying its damnedest to fulfill its promises, but which has to struggle with a traditionbound membership and a fifty-million-dollar military program in order to do so. If we look only at today, we have to ask whether we want forty cents of each dollar we contribute to support the peace and comfort of Major Smith in Berlin, when George Smith in Harlem may die tomorrow because the Red Cross blood program is inadequate.

Instead of asking us to ignore yesterday, those Red Cross employees should join us in taking a hard look at the past. There they would discover that neither Clara Barton nor the United States Congress considered the welfare of a peacetime army as part of the Red Cross mission. Of course, peacetime armies were not really in vogue then. But neither were highway deaths and blood transfusions, speedboats and water safety courses. History tells us that the Red Cross was conceived not as an arm of the Defense Department but as a civilian hospital corps. And a hospital corps takes care of sick and wounded people, not a GI who wonders whether his girlfriend is fooling around back in the States. Filling that kind of need simply lets the Defense Department off the hook while diverting our civilian hospital corps from the peacetime wounded who need its help.

Most of the Red Cross employees I interviewed seem to realize that there are indeed vast numbers of peacetime wounded out there who need Red Cross help. They tell me that their organization is not reaching all the people it should, and they fear that in the future the challenges will grow and that the Red Cross resources to meet those challenges will be insufficient. They say that the Red Cross is rapidly approaching a crossroads, not only as to its drug-abuse programs and involvement in the inner city but also with regard to two of its most basic programs: blood and disaster relief.

There is little doubt that our nation will be facing a very real blood crisis during the next few years. The problem arises from a complex mélange of fact, emotion, and politics. There are three sources of blood in the United States: the Red Cross, the American Association of Blood Banks (AABB) membership, and commercial blood banks. From the consumer's point of view, the major difference among these sources is where the blood is obtained. The Red Cross uses only volunteer donors, AABB members use both volunteer and paid donors, and commercial banks use entirely paid donors. The distinction is much more than monetary. The chances of contracting hepatitis from paid blood are ten times greater than from donated blood. Over the past few years, this danger has been brought to the public's attention in dramatic fashion, through books and television documentaries—and lawmakers are now beginning to react.

In Illinois, for example, former Governor Richard Ogilvie, who once contracted hepatitis himself from transfused blood, effected passage of a 1972 blood-labeling act. It requires each unit of blood used in Illinois to have a label that discloses whether the blood was obtained from a paid or a volunteer source. Because of the proven dangers of paid blood, the act will require every Illinois doctor and hospital either to use volunteer blood or to risk an open-and-shut malpractice suit for using paid blood. We can expect other state legislatures throughout the country to follow Illinois and pass similar statutes.

This means that, during the next few years, we will be shifting to an all-volunteer blood supply. The question is who will do the supplying. There are many reasons for turning to the Red Cross. It has the capability of meeting the need. It can attract more donors, process more blood, and distribute more units than any other organization in the country. It is estimated that today the Red Cross provides about half the nation's supply, with AABB membership providing the lion's share of the rest (between 30 and 40 per cent). The Red Cross can do the job more cheaply than other suppliers because of the volunteer talent it uses and its mass-distribution techniques. Perhaps most important, the Red Cross is the only supplier that views blood as a community responsibility rather than an individual one. The others require the recipient either to replace the blood he or she receives, or pay for it. All suppliers, including the Red Cross, charge a hospital service fee, which is usually passed on to the recipient and picked up by health insurance.

Blood means charity in its classic sense—a personal tithe that most of us can spare and many of us will someday need. As Richard Titmuss so cogently points out in *The Gift Relationship* (Pantheon, 1971), commercializing either end of the blood transaction leads to an erosion of human faith and social consciousness, to a public's loss of confidence in its own charitable nature. By the same token, a government-controlled blood program would certainly cast some dark shadows on the future of private American charity and its ability to cope with today's social needs. And yet, this is a very real possibility if dramatic action is not soon taken to fill our volunteer blood-supply need.

Whether the Red Cross will meet this impending challenge raises a distressing line of thought. It begins with the realization that our blood system has been less than ideal for some time. It continues with the confession by Red Cross executives that they knew the crisis was coming. And it ends with the undeniable fact that the Red Cross has moved not an inch to broaden its blood program. Why? The most obvious reason is that the military-services program, coupled with those skyrocketing disaster-relief costs, has allowed the organization no resources with which to broaden anything. There is a second reason. "There are a hell of a lot of powerful people who have their own fish to fry," a Red Cross executive told me. "They want to keep our blood program right where it is." Owners of commercial blood banks, pathologists getting high salaries or consultant fees, executives of commercial and AABB banks—all have strong vested interests in the *status quo*. Red Cross policy in the past has been to avoid stepping on such well-connected toes. The question, of course, is whether the organization will choose toe saving or lifesaving before the blood crisis is upon us. Mutual back scratching may be a popular business pastime for the typical Red Cross volunteer, but it has no place in the charity world.

Similar forces are at work in the disaster-relief program. Over the years, there have been numerous complaints, such as those evolving from the Mississippi tornado, that the Red Cross has been slow to respond to disasters that strike poorer areas, particularly black neighborhoods in the Deep South. Red Cross volunteers have been accused of haughtiness and lack of compassion during disasters. One survey taken several years ago after a Michigan disaster showed disaster victims rating the Salvation Army more favorably than the Red Cross, even though the latter organization provided a great deal more assistance.

Red Cross officials attribute this to unconscious scapegoating—the organization most visible during a calamity is bound to become the target of a victim's sorrow, anxiety, and frustration. There is no way to disprove such a theory. But one cannot help feeling that at least part of the problem is again attributable to the Red Cross volunteer. George Elsey admitted as much when he told me that racial tension contributed to his organization's poor showing in Mississippi. It seems reasonable to expect some difficulties when Lady Bountiful emerges from her mansion to help those poor creatures down the hill.

An equally serious problem involves the division of disaster-relief responsibility between the government sector and the private one. One reason behind the issuance of the Red Cross Congressional charter in 1900 was the unwillingness of the federal government to enter the disaster-relief field or any relief field, for that matter. But things changed a bit during the 1930s and by the middle of the following decade, the Red Cross had become most concerned. A 1946 Red Cross report warned that "clouds are appearing on the disaster relief horizon" in the form of increasing governmental participation and warned the organization to "be on the alert at all times" to check such a trend. This came at a time when the Red Cross, under Basil O'Connor's direction, was striving to expand its authority and when it certainly had the means to do so. Its disaster-relief program involved two phases of activity: an initial rescue mission during the disaster and financial aid to victims afterward. It was in the latter phase that the government was beginning to show an interest. And, although wisdom increases dramatically with retrospect, Red Cross officials probably should have realized that they had bitten off a bit more than they could chew and that it was in their best interests to cut the government in on the ground floor and clearly define responsibilities. But that would have been contrary to accepted principles of empire building and it would have smacked of "creeping socialism" as well.

Since then, the Red Cross has had a change of heart. The reason becomes obvious with one glance at the past few annual reports. In 1969 the Red Cross spent $9 million on disaster relief; in 1970, $32 million; in 1971, $25 million;

and in 1972, with the bills still coming in, $20 million. In three years, disaster costs have wiped out Red Cross emergency reserves and driven the organization to the brink of financial ruin. Under such pressure, the Red Cross decided to support legislation, passed in 1972, that has all but eliminated the second phase of its disaster program. Henceforth, the federal government will provide nearly all financial assistance to disaster victims. And according to Red Cross officials, even this major governmental participation has relieved only part of the strain. The Red Cross is critically overextended, scrambling desperately for funds. With the lines still vaguely drawn, with the Red Cross on the defensive, with an ever-hungry governmental bureaucracy close at its heels, there is a very real danger that the Red Cross disaster-relief program will be gobbled up entirely. If it does fail, a lot of talent, experience, and manpower will go with it, along with a lot of faith in our ability to help ourselves without governmental interference.

It can happen. Indeed, Red Cross history shows us how and why it can happen. When Clara Barton and her charity pioneers decided to go respectable, they failed to realize that true charity—deep-down, gut charity—is actually a pretty disreputable commodity among some very reputable segments of the community. Charity too often ends at the railroad tracks, or where political influence begins, or where it would interfere with someone's profit. When the Red Cross, under Basil O'Connor's direction, decided to climb in bed with the Defense Department in order to justify its own existence, it failed to realize that it was encumbering itself not only with an expensive program of questionable charitable value, but also with the paraphernalia of wartime patriotism that can easily obscure the demands of peacetime social need. When our civilian hospital corps fashioned itself into a great bureaucracy, it failed to realize it was entering a world of dubious sanity, where vast empires engage in mortal combat to gain control of one more piece of turf regardless of whether they are capable of administering it.

I have an idea: Suppose George Elsey and his associates were to rethink the Red Cross mission and conclude that Clara Barton's original concept was right, after all. What would happen? The most obvious consequence would be the elimination of the military-services program, freeing $50 million and several thousand employees for expansion of the blood and disaster-relief programs. The Red Cross staff would now be able to face, indeed would be forced to face, such questions as whether there is as much Red Cross blood available in Harlem as there is in Westchester. If not, there would no longer be an excuse for failing to rectify the situation or for failing to establish the drug-abuse programs that are well within the mission of a modern civilian hospital corps. Stating the organization's mission in these clear terms and eliminating the white and blue from the Red Cross would undoubtedly be a big help in attracting the blacks and young people that Red Cross officials say they want and need. After all, how many of those people are going to rush to a convention in order to hear two army generals and a business executive?

If we looked just at that white-pillared building or at the glossy photographs that adorn its corridors, my idea would seem a hopeless dream. But there are people behind those doors—people such as George Elsey, Dick Bjuberg, and Edwin Powers, people who do seem to care. They are the signs of hope. If they care enough, they will fashion something wonderful from what has been wonderful only at times. And we will all be grateful.

8   Charity Gone Sour

Brett moved close to me. We sat close against each other, I put my arm around her and she rested against me comfortably. It was very hot and bright, and the houses looked sharply white. We turned out onto the Gran Via.

"Oh, Jake," Brett said, "we could have had such a damned good time together."

Ahead was a mounted policeman in khaki directing traffic. He raised his baton. The car slowed suddenly pressing Brett against me.

"Yes," I said. "Isn't it pretty to think so?"[1]

It leaves a ghastly picture: the bright sunshine; Jake Barnes with his war wound and Lady Brett Ashley with her passions, apparently in love and at peace in the back seat of a

[1] *The Sun Also Rises,* by Ernest Hemingway (Scribner's, 1926), p. 247.

Madrid taxi cab, but actually grinding away in frustration at impossible dreams and bitter reality.

Nearly a half century later, I am sitting here holding the 1970 golden-anniversary report of the Disabled American Veterans (DAV). The report has a gold cover and gold lettering. It says "Fifty Years of Service" at the top. Inside, there is a gold-tinted photograph of Richard Nixon and a gold-tinted reproduction of a letter he wrote dated May 6, 1970. The letter says in part: "Our nation is stronger and our heritage safer because of your determination. And your patriotism is an example to all of us. By your sacrifices you have indeed made the five decades of your history golden years for our country. Your service can never be forgotten and it will strengthen and inspire men and women for generations to come."

On the next page, there are similar endorsements from celebrities, past and present. The DAV even managed to get a few words from Calvin Coolidge. And then comes a six-page historical narrative. It begins just after World War I, and it relates how that war produced three hundred thousand American wounded. Medical facilities were insufficient to cope with the deluge. The government had compensation programs and vocational training programs for veterans. But facilities were inadequate, administration inefficient.

The DAV narrative relates how, on Christmas Day in 1919, Judge Robert Marx of Cincinnati, Ohio, gave a party for one hundred of his fellow disabled veterans. The party turned into a meeting at which problems of disabled veterans were discussed, and the meeting concluded with a resolution to form a national organization that would represent the interests of disabled veterans. Marx traveled the nation enlisting support for the idea and, less than two years later, one thousand delegates attended the DAV's first national convention, in Detroit. During the convention, Marx led a parade of his fellow DAV members through the streets. The narrative says: "It was a parade of people, some of whom coughed violently from TB, some hobbled unsteadily on new limbs, blind men were led by those who could see better and those who could not walk rode in cars or wheelchairs. The parade was escorted by the police and a troop of cavalry— and it was raining."

The narrative goes on to say that the DAV obtained a Congressional charter on June 17, 1932, proclaiming the organization "the official voice of the nation's wartime disabled." It describes the organization's growth from the seventeen thousand members it had in 1922 to the nearly three hundred thousand in 1970. The narrative ends: ". . . it has determinedly stuck to its single purpose—that of aiding the wartime service connected disabled veteran return to civilian life in a competitive position with his peers. That he and his family can face the future with confidence knowing that his medical, rehabilitation and employment requirements will be met. No greater purpose can be served by any organization—no greater challenge can be accepted by any group—no greater privilege is requested by the Disabled American Veterans."

It is a bit overdone, of course. But we expect such things in the charity world and, all in all, that golden-anniversary report creates a convincing picture of a golden charity investment; endorsed by Richard Nixon and Calvin Coolidge, serving the interests of America's victims with steel-jawed determination. On the other hand, we have already learned that Jake Barnes and Brett Ashley do not hold an exclusive claim on deceiving appearances. American charity has more than its share of illusions and mismatches. And, looking more closely at the gold-covered report, we find plenty of reason to believe that all is not what it seems to be in the back seat of the DAV.

Near the end of the report, there is a 1969 financial statement. It reveals that the DAV raised $10.2 million in contributions during that year. Of this amount, over $5.9 million, nearly 58 per cent of receipts, went for fund raising alone. High fund-raising cost as we have seen, are justifiable in a variety of ways. None of them applies here. By 1969 the DAV had been in business for fifty years, sporting presidential endorsements and one of the most potent charitable causes on the market. By 1969 the DAV had been engaged in direct-mail fund raising for twenty-eight years, which is a lot of time to build reliable mailing lists and an efficient fund-raising enterprise. The DAV had not done so. The reasons for this failure are not set out in the anniversary report. In fact, the narrative paints its golden picture around, through, and over those fund-raising costs without even acknowledging their existence. In order to understand where they came from, we must look at events, attitudes, and names that are not part of the DAV's official certified history, but which did and do exist nevertheless, no matter how pretty it might be to think otherwise. The most significant name of all is, of course, that of Abraham Koolish.

When Koolish joined forces with the DAV in 1941, he was not exactly an unbesmirched businessman. He had dealt in punchboards and similar paraphernalia, schemes that brought him into several unpleasant confrontations with the Federal Trade Commission. That the DAV executives would do business with such a person in the first place indicates some divergence from the organization's noble tradition. More revealing is the type of fund-raising enterprise that Koolish was hired to direct. The organization could have solicited funds through direct mail on the basis of its cause alone. After all, we were launching the greatest and most moral war in our history. And that was what the DAV was about. But it rejected such a course and, instead, chose the ident-o-tag.

I remember, as a child, noticing one of those miniature license plates on my father's key ring and asking him about it. He told me that if he lost his keys and a nice person found them, the keys would be put in the mailbox and eventually returned to him. It was a service provided by a charity to which he gave money. I thought about it for a while and, being a somewhat cynical kid, I went back to my father and asked him what would happen if his keys were found by a nasty person, who could look at the little license plate and learn which car the keys belonged to and maybe even learn where we live and use the keys to get into our house. My father looked at me and didn't answer. The next day, the license tag was gone from his key ring.

There were much more serious reasons for DAV officials to reject the ident-o-tag. Although it was a worthless gimmick in itself, it was tied to a service that might easily be viewed as valuable by potential contributors. What Koolish had in mind is obvious: wringing out contributions for the DAV (and for Abraham Koolish) by imposing guilt feelings and a sense of obligation on the potential contributor. And DAV officials bought it. They also bought a very expensive fund-raising enterprise. Koolish charged the organization $62.50 for every thousand solicitation letters he mailed out. In 1943, he mailed out over eight million letters, which means he was paid five hundred thousand dollars by the DAV (over $2 million by today's standards). The organization's income that year, after deducting fees and fund-raising expenses, was about three hundred thousand.

In 1945 the DAV purchased the ident-o-tag enterprise from Koolish for $1.3 million. Since the ident-o-tag is a non-patentable gimmick that the DAV could have used itself without Abraham Koolish, the price seems a bit high. The organization also hired Koolish as a consultant to oversee the fund-raising operation at a monthly retainer fee of one thousand dollars. In 1945 government attorneys were receiving salaries of slightly over two hundred fifty dollars a month. But, then, they did not have a fund-raising gimmick and they were not working for the DAV.

The departure of Abraham Koolish for greener charity pastures did not have much of an impact on DAV fund raising. In 1963, the year Koolish was convicted of the Sister Kenny fraud, DAV receipts were $3.3 million and fund-raising costs $2.9 million, or an astounding 88 per cent of receipts. There were other indications that Abraham Koolish had departed in body only. A 1954 study by the New York Legislature into charity fund raising had revealed that the DAV, like Koolish's National Kids Day, had been using endorsements of military officers without permission. A 1958 investigation by a Congressional committee into veterans' organizations had concluded that Vivian Corbly, national adjutant of the DAV, had been buying gift merchandise for the DAV with DAV funds from a company called Raybill, Incorporated. The company was owned by Vivian Corbly. Corbly denied impropriety, but resigned in the wake of these and other revelations.

The most astounding aspect of the Corbly incident is the reaction of the DAV membership. Despite revelations of Corbly's insider dealing, despite his resignation, the membership decided not only to give him a vote of confidence, but also to keep him on the payroll for two years after he resigned, so that he would be entitled to a DAV pension. This cost DAV contributors a total of thirty-six thousand dollars, not including employee benefits or the cost of Corbly's pension itself. It was a brazen act of nose-thumbing. It revealed that the DAV membership did not give a damn

about the contributors who were pouring money into the
DAV. And it indicated there was more Koolishness to come.
There was indeed.

In 1961, a few months after Vivian Corbly received his
last bonus check from the DAV, the organization entered
into a fund-raising contract with Colonel Harold S. McClintock. Pursuant to that agreement, the DAV set up a new
fund-raising program, called Operation Rehabilitation, which
was designed to attract gifts of property from big corporations. The property would then be sold and the proceeds
split fifty-fifty between McClintock and the DAV, after
McClintock deducted his expenses. The DAV gave McClintock the official title of National Director of Operation Rehabilitation and official stationery to go with it. This meant that
the good colonel was provided with the appearance of a devoted DAV servant, certified as a responsible DAV official,
given all the trappings of a direct conduit to an apparently
worthwhile charity. In reality, he was an outside entrepreneur
with a contractual inducement to be as irresponsible as he
wished in obtaining donations, which inducement included
hiding the fact that half of every contribution was going, not
to the DAV, but into his own pocket.

In 1967 one of McClintock's hired solicitors filed suit
against the DAV in federal district court in Washington,
D.C. (*Rice* v. *Disabled American Veterans*, C.A. 2018–
67). The court papers tell an interesting story, which DAV
officials confirmed in depositions. In 1967, after the DAV
had received over two million dollars from Operation Rehabilitation, DAV officials were advised by the Illinois state
attorney general that McClintock's real name was Harold
Sager and that he had been defrauding not only DAV contributors, but the DAV as well. It seems that a 50 per cent
cut of the take was not quite enough for the National Director of Operation Rehabilitation, and he simply kept over a

million dollars in DAV contributions himself, without reporting it to the organization.

In their depositions, national adjutant Denvel Adams and
other DAV officials claimed that they, like the contributors
who gave McClintock-Sager the property that he did not
report, were innocent victims of the scheme. But they did
admit that McClintock-Sager had been an off-and-on DAV
fund raiser since 1948, that he was associated with a past
national commander of the DAV, that he had indeed been
given an official title and DAV stationery, and that Adams
had assigned a member of his personal staff to the fund-
raising operation as a liaison. In his deposition, Denvel
Adams stated that he had suspected McClintock-Sager of
being up to no good for some time before he was contacted
by the Illinois attorney general. But he admitted that he had
made no move to terminate the arrangement. Other DAV
officials testified that no effort was made to audit Operation
Rehabilitation books or check on its activities. Finally Adams testified that, even after McClintock-Sager was sent
packing, Operation Rehabilitation was continued with other
solicitors, although the name of the program was changed.
The enterprise has since been discontinued.

Throughout this shabby affair, the DAV's primary fund-
raising effort remained direct-mail solicitation and the ident-
o-tag. By steadily increasing its mail blitz, the organization
managed to attract more and more contributions: $8.2 mil-
lion in 1967, $10 million in 1968, $10.2 million in 1969,
$12 million in 1970, and a mind-boggling $20.8 million in
1971. While fund-raising costs decreased percentage wise
during those years, from 70 per cent in 1970 to slightly under 50 per cent in 1971, they remained shockingly high.
They were also somewhat unpredictable, dropping to 58
per cent of contributions in 1969, rising to 63 per cent of
contributions in 1970, and dropping again in 1971. These

statistics were also somewhat misleading. In 1970, for example, stated fund-raising costs of $7.6 million did not include public-relations costs of $67,000, a $58,500 claim settlement arising from a fund-raising enterprise, the $33,500 cost of returning lost keys to motorists or $73,000 in professional fees (most of which were legal costs of defending five lawsuits arising from fund-raising enterprises).

All considered, the three decades of DAV direct-mail fund raising comprise a long and rather shameful chapter in the history of American charity. It would be comforting to pretend it never happened, or to write it off as some sort of aberration, or to excuse it through the ends-justify-means approach that we often find in the charity world. But Ernest Hemingway's favorite theme seems more than a little fitting here: reality continues unchanged no matter how hard you try to deny it or glamorize it. And the reality is that the DAV adopted a high-priced fund-raising gimmick thirty years ago which it has failed to abandon. The reality is that DAV has used two fund raisers who have since been convicted of fraud. The reality is that the DAV is very much in existence today. But the cruelest truth of all is that fund raising is not the worst of it; Abraham Koolish, Harold McClintock-Sager, and the ident-o-tag were, in fact, only surface reflections of the deeply flawed organization that lay beneath them.

In 1970, in addition to the $7.6 million in acknowledged fund-raising costs, the DAV financial statement lists four expenditure categories: Free Service to All Veterans and Members, Special Service to Members, Free Service to Motorists, and General Service to Veterans and Members. The Service to Motorists is the returning of lost keys, the $33,500 expense mentioned previously. The General Service to Veterans and Members category is defined as "supervision of all activities and maintenance of records" at the

DAV national headquarters in Cold Springs, Kentucky. This category accounted for $2.5 million in DAV funds in 1970, and it included the claims settlement, the professional fees, public-relations costs, and the salaries of Denvel Adams and his staff. Apparently, Adams did not see fit to allocate national headquarters costs among "all activities." So the $2.5 million must include a little fund raising, a little service to veterans, a little service to members, and so forth. The most significant item in the Special Service to Members category is the cost of publishing the DAV monthly magazine, at about three hundred thousand dollars. There are also minor costs for mailing the magazine.

This leaves Free Service to All Veterans and Members, which the DAV likes to call its "chartered purpose." This category includes three activities: counseling veterans on how to obtain government benefits, lobbying for more veterans' benefits, and throwing an annual national convention. The counseling service cost about $1.4 million, the lobbying program about $83,000, and the convention about $101,000. There is also an item labeled "expenses of National Commander and staff." The National Commander is pretty much a figurehead who presides at national conventions.

If we sift through these expenditures in search of a reasonable charitable purpose, most of that $12.2 million in contributions flows right down the drain. Those $7.6 million in fund-raising costs certainly don't make much of a worthy cause. Nor does a membership magazine or a national convention. Which leaves a tiny lump of money for DAV lobbying and a larger one for counseling services. In this age of military retirement benefits, military disability benefits, free hospital service, commissary benefits, and such, lobbying on behalf of veterans seems more like gilding an overflowing pot than filling an alms plate.

Just for the sake of argument, though, let us put that $83,000 lobbying cost in the charitable-purpose column anyway. The veterans' counseling service consists of maintaining a DAV representative at each Veterans Administration office around the country—about one hundred fifty in all. These representatives counsel veterans on how to fill out Veterans Administration claim forms. It seems a worthwhile activity. The only difficulty is that the government employs its own counselors to provide exactly the same service. In addition, more than sixty private organizations maintain their own counselors at Veterans Administration offices to provide exactly the same service. A Veterans Administration official told me that the counselors from all these organizations do a competent job. A representative of one organization that provides this service told me that his counselors receive considerable business from veterans who had tried the DAV and found its service unsatisfactory.

Competence aside, the DAV representatives can point to several characteristics that distinguish them from others engaged in the same activity. Theirs is the only organization that solicits funds from the public on the grounds of a service provided by the government and sixty other organizations. And taking fund raising and general administration into account, theirs is the only organization that charged its supporters twelve million dollars for two million dollars' worth of counseling services in 1970. But we'll put that $1.4 million into the charitable-purpose column anyway and add in $361,000 for the stenographic services provided to DAV counselors and $168,000 in employees' benefits (all these figures have been rounded out in the DAV's favor). Our charitable-purpose column now contains a grand total of $2,012,000, which is not really so grand when compared with total DAV contributions ($12 million). It means that in 1970, if you contributed to the DAV, slightly more than sixteen cents of every dollar you gave went for a purpose that was even remotely charitable in nature. In 1971, this amount dropped below fifteen cents.

The official history set out in the DAV golden-anniversary report mentions none of these things, of course. But a photograph in the report seems to prove that Judge Robert Marx did, in fact, exist and that he did lead a band of disabled veterans down the streets of Detroit. However, contrary to the claim of the DAV historian, the photograph establishes —through bright sunshine and clear-cut shadows—that it was not raining at the time. And the only evidence of disability in the photograph is one man walking with a cane. But I am certainly willing, even eager, to believe that Judge Marx was sincerely committed to helping the plight of the disabled veteran. There is certainly no doubt that at the time Marx began building his organization, there was much to set straight.

Shortly after the Civil War, when veterans became sufficiently numerous to be considered political footballs, politicians began falling over each other to promise more and more veterans' benefits. When these politicians attained office, they fulfilled those promises by passing incredible legislation, presumably designed to aid veterans, but actually shoddy laws that worked more in aid of fraud and corruption. The Arrears-of-Pension Act, passed by Congress in 1879, granted back pay to anyone who could prove an injury from a war that had ended fourteen years earlier. Around this Act, there arose a new class of pension lawyers, who actually sought out potential claimants, legitimate and otherwise. The pension lawyers undoubtedly benefited as much as the veterans, perhaps more.

It become more and more fashionable for congressmen to serve their veteran constituents by effecting passage of special bills that granted individuals pensions that they may or may not have deserved in fact and law. During Grover Cleveland's administration alone, Congress passed *two thousand* such bills. Cleveland determined that many of these bills were based on fraudulent claims and vetoed them. He also vetoed the Dependent Pension Bill, which would have granted a pension to any disabled person who had served at least three months in the Civil War. The disability did not have to be connected to wartime or even military service. If you broke a leg in 1887 and could prove three months of Civil War service twenty-two years earlier, you would have been entitled to a pension under the bill. Cleveland's veto of this ridiculous legislation earned him considerable unpopularity.

After the First World War, veterans' interests directed heavy pressure at Congress to pass bigger and bigger pension bills. Congress usually responded. In fact, it overresponded, nearly passing a two-billion-dollar pension bill right in the middle of the Depression, a bill that the American Legion itself had declared unwise in view of the national economic crisis. The problem was less the amount of money authorized than the fact that too little of this amount was reaching veterans, due to inefficient and corrupt administration. The difficulty was apparently solved by the creation of a new governmental agency—the Veterans Bureau—under which all veterans' services were consolidated. Warren Harding appointed a man named Charles Forbes to head the new agency. Less than a year later, Forbes resigned his post, and he was soon after convicted of defrauding the government and sentenced to two years imprisonment. It was in the wake of such legislative insanity and administrative chicanery that Robert Marx founded the DAV. There is, then, no reason to doubt that he was motivated by a pure heart to meet a real challenge. The obvious question is, What went wrong?

Several factors seem to have been at work in the souring of the DAV. For one thing, it is more than a little apparent from our brief look at American history that the cause of veterans' benefits does not exactly lend itself to sound judgment on any side. The welfare of our heroes automatically produces a deep and blindly emotional reaction, inextricably entwined with patriotism and good citizenship, inevitably infecting non-veterans with guilt feelings and a sense of obligation toward those who risked their necks in wartime. For the veterans who spent four years in foxholes and maybe lost a limb or an eye as a result, there is the understandable feeling that the public's obligation to repay them for their sacrifices is limitless. In the governmental sphere, the interaction of these human attitudes produced the Dependent Pension Bill. In the charity world, it helped forge the Koolish-DAV partnership, which was certainly the most significant event in modern DAV history.

What Abraham Koolish saw in the DAV was a means to exploit human weakness to his advantage through an enterprise that would not bring him into another unpleasant contact with the Federal Trade Commission. For Koolish, it was necessary to work both sides of the charity transaction. He had to convince DAV officials to adopt his rather shabby fund-raising techniques and allow him full use of the DAV as a front organization. And he had to convince potential contributions to part with their hard-earned cash. The emotional aura that surrounds the question of veterans' benefits—of how much we owe our veterans and of how much they expect from us—made Koolish's job rather easy at both ends. And in attracting money from contributors, the Koolish direct-mail genius (minus the arrogance that was primarily responsible for his later undoing) worked beautifully in emphasizing the emotion, the guilt feelings, and the sense of obligation, to a vulnerable public.

Until Abraham Koolish came along, the DAV was always scraping around for a dollar. Its members were standing on street corners, handing out little red poppies in exchange for contributions. Like beggars. Koolish relieved them of the burden. So what if it took $800,000 in contributions to net $300,000 in DAV funds? That was still $200,000 more than the organization was getting from poppy sales. So what if Koolish got the lion's share of receipts? He had a right to make a living. And so the DAV altered course.

Once on the path of Koolishness, various factors worked to deepen the DAV's misdirection. For one thing, the money was remarkably easy to acquire. Here was a charitable organization that was making no pretense of devoting even part of its money to research grants or CARE packages. It did not bother to round up volunteers for door-to-door solicitations. For the most part, its public visibility was limited to a solicitation letter and an annual convention. Its contributing public never demanded that the DAV prove its worth. The ident-o-tag arrived in the mail, the letter said, "Help disabled veterans," and the money flowed in.

The DAV of the post-Koolish era was attracting just the sort of member who would succumb to such temptations without a terribly violent rebellion of conscience. Less than twenty years before, disabled veterans had been driven out of the nation's capital by police, after refusing to abandon their protest encampment. In fact, it was under pressure of the encamped protesters that Congress issured the DAV charter. But now, the military and business establishments were rapidly becoming interchangeable. Postwar industry was booming and military personnel were flowing into the business world, where their Pentagon connections were convertible to big government contracts. And we have already seen that some of the worst evils of the charity world are fashioned by attitudes that have been imported from American business.

Defenders of the DAV claim that there is, in effect, a counterbalance to these forces (which they deny exist) in the annual audit conducted by the General Accounting Office (GAO). They say that if the DAV were playing fast and loose with contributors' money, the GAO would find out about it and put an end to it. And they intimate that the GAO annual audit report is akin to the *Good Housekeeping* Seal of Approval. Without commenting on the efficacy of that type of endorsement, suffice it to say that the GAO audit provides absolutely no assurance of DAV propriety. The GAO makes very clear at the beginning of each report that its examination is limited to the financial statements prepared by DAV accountants, that it neither considers nor comments on what the DAV is, says, or does, and that it accepts DAV financial data at their face value without question. This is not to say that the GAO is responsible for the Koolishness or the high fund-raising costs. Its authority is limited and its other responsibilities are considerable. It is simply unfortunate that the law creates a situation in which the GAO assumes the appearance of a watchdog when it actually is not, an appearance that can be made to mislead potential contributors.

The truth is that the DAV is the least public and least scrutinized member of our least regulated and most permissive business system, American charity. This is so by reason of one extraordinary fact about the nature of the DAV: although supported almost entirely by public funds, it is not a public organization. It is a private membership association to which the great majority of us cannot gain admittance. And even those who are entitled to join, and who do apply and pay their dues, do not receive an unconditional membership. According to DAV bylaws, any member can be "blacklisted" for some unspecified act that displeases the membership. What, then, are the chances of someone from that already narrow-viewed, closed-membership society standing up at a national convention and berating his fellow members for ripping off the American contributor?

Several hundred thousand dollars in public contributions are used each year to finance the DAV national convention. At its golden-anniversary convention, held in Detroit during August 1971, the DAV devoted a considerable portion of its publicly financed time to considering fourteen resolutions that concerned, not the health and welfare of disabled veterans, but Richard Nixon's Viet Nam policy. The resolutions had been drafted in advance by the Pentagon. Department of Defense officials told reporters that the DAV had requested their help.

From 1967 through 1971, the American public donated $61.3 million to support the activities of this private-membership association. Had this amount been channeled into more publicly oriented organizations, it would have supported 42,500 overseas orphans for the next ten years, or paid the research bills of the Muscular Dystrophy Association for the next fifteen years, or completely financed the American Social Health Association's fight against venereal disease for the next sixty years.

Furthermore, there are countless private-membership associations in America that do not pose as charities, that do not request public support for their private activities and thereby divert the charitable dollar from true charitable purposes. For example, the American Automobile Association (AAA) is a membership organization that represents the interests of another victim of our society—the American motorist. Without judging how well it does its job, we can certainly give the AAA credit for supporting itself on membership dues alone and for not holding out its hand to the general public. And yet, it provides the same types of services for its members that DAV members receive from their organization. It lobbies for them, it publishes a magazine for them, and it offers them discount insurance packages. It does not, however, throw an annual convention.

During the past few years, the DAV has been attempting to add at least the appearance of renewed vitality to its purpose by establishing special funds and giving out grants to the Boy Scouts of America (another private-membership association posing as a charity). Through 1970, a grand total of slightly over $100,000 in DAV funds had been allocated to the DAV disaster-relief fund, its scholarship fund, and the Boy Scouts.[2] Other DAV funds fared considerably better. By the end of 1970, the DAV operating fund held over $8 million in net assets. Another $8 million in assets was held by the DAV service foundation. The DAV 1971 annual report reveals that a total of $5.8 million was left over from that year's contributions, for which even the spendthrift DAV was unable to find a parking place. This excess amount went into the operating fund, raising its balance to almost $14 million. If the DAV did not mail out one solicitation letter next year, it would nevertheless receive about $3 million: over $1 million in dues; $200,000 in rental income; $400,000 from mailing-list rentals; and, of course, interest on that $14 million, which is a lot of interest. This income would easily pay for DAV counseling services and lobbying.

The $1 million that the DAV receives annually in dues comes from over three hundred thousand members who pay a mere three dollars apiece each year. By simply increasing those annual dues to twenty dollars, the DAV

[2] It is, of course, inherently ridiculous to donate to an organization because it gives some of your money to another organization to which you could contribute directly.

would acquire enough money to run itself completely without imposing on the American contributor. Is twenty dollars too high a price to charge a DAV member for his private, special-interest organization? If it is, then twenty million dollars is certainly too high a price to charge American contributors. We have nevertheless been picking up the tab. We have been paying the convention bills, the fund-raising bills, and the public-relations bills. We have been paying the legal fees arising from those dubious fund-raising enterprises. We have, in fact, been financing our own exploitation by people who have repeatedly demonstrated their disdain for us and for the principles by which we expect American charity to function.

9   The Quiet Charity

The lunchtime crowd seethed along Fifth Avenue—a cater-pillar train of people in mad motion. They trickled into the side streets, picking up speed; dodged the delivery carts and occasionally darted across the path of a honking taxi. The frenzy seemed to increase with each passing moment. The revolving doors spun faster. The taxis honked louder. The pedestrians moved with wilder and wilder abandon. I was sure that this time the laws of nature would fail us. The city would fall apart at the seams; the island would break loose from its moorings and spin off crazily into the ocean. But I was wrong. The sidewalk stayed firmly beneath me as I turned west onto Fifty-sixth Street and headed for number 33.

There are several buildings like number 33 on the same block: old mansions and town houses, some dating back a half century and more. Most of them are no longer stately. They bear the gaudy marks of various commercial enterprises. And during a weekday lunch hour, they attract the noise and human turmoil that fills their cash registers. Number 33 is different. Somehow it has managed to retain the appearance of calm elegance that its builders must have had in mind when they designed its gray stone facing and large windows. But its most significant distinction lies in the fact that it is the only building in the world that houses the Damon Runyon-Walter Winchell Cancer Fund, a unique organization indeed.

In 1972 the Fund received $2 million in contributions from the general public and paid out $1.1 million in fellowship grants to cancer scientists and $1.4 million in direct cancer-research grants. It seems incredible, but for every dollar donated to the Fund for cancer research, a dollar and a quarter went for cancer research. There is certainly no better bargain anywhere in the charity world. The mechanics are actually rather simple: a separate administrative fund pays operating expenses; a theater ticket service and investments provide additional income for research. But there has to be more to it than that. Otherwise the Fund would not be the only charity of its kind. It was for this reason that I returned to 33 West Fifty-sixth Street for a second day in a row, to look for clues.

The heavy door closed behind me. It was dark and very quiet. I went through the foyer and across the marble floor. None of the lamps was lit and there was not a human being in sight. My footsteps actually echoed along the walls, and I could hear myself breathing. In earlier days this must have been the salon, and back there, the dining room. Now a plain wooden desk stood beside the ornate fireplace and there was filing cabinets where the sideboard must have been. Dorothy C. Moore, executive director of the Fund, had warned me about the lights the day before: "It's probably silly of me. But it makes me feel good to save even a penny when I can. So I go around here turning everything off."

A typewriter began clattering above me. I climbed the winding staircase. The two Fund employees who handle the theater-ticket service were behind their desks in the hallway, working by the light of desk lamps alone. They said that the other five Fund employees were out to lunch and that Miss Moore had left some information for me in the office over there. I went in and found a desk piled high with dusty scrapbooks. In a few moments, I was deeply immersed in the organization's fascinating past.

It began in the early 1920s, when a kid by the name of Walter Winchell first met the New York *Mirror* columnist Damon Runyon. Their acquaintanceship gradually developed into a friendship. In 1944 Runyon contracted cancer of the throat, and the following year his larynx was removed. After that, he and Winchell became very close. They would ride together in Winchell's car, tracking down police and fire calls from evening until dawn. Runyon had lost his voice as a result of the operation, and he communicated by scribbling messages on a note pad. One of his notes to Winchell said: "You can keep the things of bronze and stone, just give me one man to remember me just once a year." He died on December 12, 1946. Three days later, Winchell asked "Mr. and Mrs. America" to remember his friend in a rather special way.

During a radio broadcast on December 15, 1946, Winchell said: "A very good friend of mine—a great newspaper-man, Damon Runyon—was killed this week by the number two killer—cancer. Let's do something about this terrible thing. Let's fight back! Will you please send me a penny, nickel, dime, or a dollar? I will turn all your donations—no expenses deducted of any kind—over to cancer fighters."

Winchell expected to receive fifty thousand dollars, at most. But he had underestimated either the impact of his endorsement or America's love for Damon Runyon. The money poured in. And it came from some rather strange sources. Runyonesque characters would "pssst" at Winchell from doorways. "Lay this C-note on the cancer thing," one told him, slipping him a bill. "Whose name should I put it under?" Winchell asked him. "Never mind," he was told. "Just put it down from synonomous." Joseph "Socks" Lanza, once the labor boss of the Fulton Fish Market, sent Winchell a contribution from prison. A covering note from Lanza's lawyer said: "Socks would be glad to raise much more if it could be arranged for him to circulate more freely."

The money was a problem. Caught unawares by the deluge, the only parking place Winchell could initially find for the donations was the American Cancer Society. In a way, this was hedging a bit on Winchell's initial promise to turn those dimes and dollars over to the "cancer fighters," presumably the research scientists, with "no expenses of any kind deducted." The Cancer Society was allocating only a quarter of its contributions for research at the time, the rest going for fund raising, administration, and, depending on your point of view, either public education or fund-raising scare campaigns. Equally serious, the Post Office Department advised Winchell that it doubted the propriety of his personal solicitation and handling of charitable contributions, even though he was actually only a funnel to a reputable organization. So he incorporated the Damon Runyon Memorial

Fund for Cancer Research. And now he really did bring
that no-expenses-deducted promise to full fruition, by arranging for the Walter Winchell Foundation to pay all
operating expenses of his new charity.[1] About the same time,
he made it known that the Runyon Fund would be allocating its donations directly to research scientists.

Walter Winchell was certainly not the first financial
angel of the charity world. The 1945 fund-raising drive that
catapulted the struggling American Cancer Society to star-
dom had been conceived and totally financed by Mary
Lasker. She suggested employing New York's super fund
raiser, John Price Jones, and she agreed to pay all his fees
and expenses, on one condition: that at least 25 per cent of
the proceeds from his efforts be allocated to cancer research.
The Cancer Society agreed, and, that year, its contributors
got a major fund-raising campaign free of charge. It stands
to reason that most, if not all, American charities owe their
existence to a handful of big financial backers. It costs a lot
of money to solicit donations from the general public, and
the money must come from somewhere. Even after a charity
is well launched, it will continue to maintain strong ties to
financial angels of various stripes: benefactors, big contributors, foundations. Most charitable organizations could not
survive without those large sums of cheaply raised money.
In a general sense, Winchell was no different from the
thousands of wealthy supporters—most of them much more
wealthy than he—who were allocating a portion of their
surplus to charitable causes. But the concept he initiated with
the establishment of the Runyon Fund set him very much
apart.

In nearly every charitable organization, the financial angels
are the ones who designate exactly where their contributions

[1] This role was later assumed by an administrative fund, supported
by Winchell, other philanthropists, and investment income.

are to applied, while the average contributor bears the burden of paying operating costs. Legally, I suppose that you and I have the right to impose whatever conditions we wish on our donations. But the sums we contribute are so small and our knowledge of a charity's activities is so limited that this right is illusory, and few small contributors bother to exercise it. Thus, if administration is inefficient or corrupt, we are the ones who are victimized. The wealthy benefactor's pet project continues unmolested.

From a public viewpoint, this situation makes no sense whatsoever. The big contributors are usually intimately involved with the organization. We are not. They hold the power to effect removal of a corrupt executive or institute better management techniques. We do not. By insulating their contributions from operating costs, however, they eliminate a major reason for personal concern and leave the executives plenty of room to misspend the money of a distant public. Quite the opposite is true with the Runyon Fund. When he created the organization, Walter Winchell cranked into its design an assurance of propriety and efficiency. It was his own money, and the money of his intimate friends, that would pay the operating costs. Our contributions would automatically be designated for cancer research, without any directions or restrictions being imposed by us. That was his condition, not ours.

Winchell himself probably did not think through his unique concept in these precise terms. "It was more a personal thing with him," Dorothy Moore told me. "It was between him and Mr. and Mrs. America. He saw what was going on with other charities and he wanted no part of it. He didn't want his charity to intrude on people. He didn't want it to twist anyone's arm or frighten people. There were some pretty big charity scandals around that time. And he didn't want his friends to worry about what would happen to the contributions they gave to him."

Certain things flowed naturally from Winchell's ground rules and the resources available to him. The Walter Winchell Foundation was not richly endowed. Thus a large, highly-paid staff was out of the question for the Runyon Fund. Today, it continues to operate with a total of seven employees, several of whom have been around from the beginning. Many of them have not had a salary raise in years. They are paid a grand total of about eighty thousand dollars, which would not even meet the payroll taxes of charities with similar incomes. Even if Winchell's ground rules had allowed for door-to-door solicitations, which they probably did not, so small a staff would not have been able to organize and direct such an enterprise. Nor was there money with which to float a nationwide direct-mail solicitation. Again, such an idea might well have been considered an intrusion by Winchell. So the Runyon Fund did not speak at all through these usual channels of communication for American charity. But it did speak.

Simultaneously with his creation of the Damon Runyon Fund, Winchell announced the informal appointment of every journalist in the nation as honorary chairman of public relations. He effectively reached out to the Runyon sporting crowd by appointing Dan Parker, the well-known sports columnist, as president of the Fund. Parker at first insisted that Winchell be president. "Hell no," Winchell replied. "I've got the money. That means I'm treasurer." And he insured the devotion of Runyon's beloved Broadway by appointing celebrity columnist Leonard Lyons as vice-president. The three of them were often seen together, not only in New York but in other parts of the nation as well, enlisting support for their charity. They mentioned the Runyon Fund often in their columns and radio broadcasts.

And their associates followed suit, taking their honorary appointments to heart. The scrapbooks Dorothy Moore had left for me that day were crammed with clippings that publicized the Fund; sometimes in a headline, more often in a line or two about a famous person who was doing something or other for the organization. Usually, the columnist would follow up with a personal endorsement of his own.

For fund raising, the Runyon Fund turned to special events, usually initiated and endorsed by a celebrity from show business or sports, and always possessing a certain earthiness and free spirit which are quite apparent from the press clippings and which make you regret not being present at the function. It was as if Damon Runyon himself had stayed around to make sure he was being remembered in the proper way. Here, for example, is a ragged copy of the January 1954 issue of *Hop Up Magazine* ("hop up" meant hot rods in those days). Amid the advertisements for dual-intake manifolds and high-compression heads, there is an article entitled "Draggin' for Damon." It tells about a charity drag race held in California on September 21, 1953, in which the Runyon Fund received all gate receipts and 60 per cent of concession-stand profits. The writer reports: "Among the various hot rod groups to contribute their services were the Santa Cruz Cam Snappers, Salinas Hi-Timers, Santa Cruz Clockers, Redwood Roadsters, Peninsula Hi-Winders, the Road Knights, Watsonville Road Angels and the San Francisco Ramblers."

Remember the NBC quiz program "Who Said That?" It was quite the thing during TV's infancy, before big money (and scandals) came to the television quiz arena. As I recall, a panel of experts, backed by anchorman John Cameron Swayze, were asked to guess who had uttered a particular quotation from the previous week's news. On the frequent occasions, when all those experts did not know the answer, they would have to kick in ten bucks apiece for the Damon Runyon Memorial Fund.

The Runyon Fund's most productive association with television came through the good graces of Mr. Television himself, Milton Berle. During the early 1950s, Berle hosted a series of five annual telethons for the charity, going twenty-two hours straight on each occasion. It was here that Jerry Lewis got his first taste of telethon fund raising, appearing with Dean Martin as Berle's guest. Numerous other celebrities also hopped on the bandwagon. A thousand volunteers took turns answering phone calls, and Berle would answer two thousand calls himself during one of the marathons. He pulled in about a million dollars in contributions on each telethon.

The celebrities demonstrated time and again that the Runyon Fund was truly their first love in the charity world. The theater-ticket service was the brainchild of Richard Rodgers and the late Oscar Hammerstein II. They induced Broadway producers and theater owners to set aside a number of choice seats for the Fund, which would then be sold to the public, with a percentage of the proceeds going to the charity. Richard Rodgers and his wife remain honorary members of the Fund, along with Mrs. Hammerstein, Joe Dimaggio, Frankie Laine, Earl Wilson, Milton Berle, and many others. Jimmy Durante and Ed Sullivan have been members of the board of directors for years. Columnist Bob Considine has been intimately involved with the organization's work for as long as anyone can remember, and he has been given the official title of "Ambassador-at-Large." And from the scrapbooks, it seems that the stars of sports, show business, and journalism were engaged in a ceaseless charity campaign of balls, ball games, benefit performances, and publicity stunts—one following the other with hardly a pause—on behalf of the Runyon Fund.

The organization also came up with a rather unusual fund-raising device: an essay contest. A wealthy supporter would provide the prizes; the journalists, the publicity. Essays would have to be accompanied by a contribution in order to qualify. One year, there were five first prizes: expense-paid round trips to Europe by luxury liner. The first prize in another contest was a bungalow that had been erected right in the middle of Times Square. The house was later moved to a site of the winner's choice.

The Fund never had an official army of volunteers. It never issued a nationwide manpower appeal; not did it ever tally up the number of people who were providing it free service at any given moment. But anyone who knows how the charity business works cannot look through that pile of scrapbooks without realizing that there had to be volunteers behind the headlines, plenty of them. Special-event fund raising is a very time-consuming method of raising money. Sponsors of even the most modest event are inevitably deluged with thousands of problems that must be resolved before, during, and after an event. The Runyon Fund hired no outside consultants to manage its fund raisers. It had a paid staff of six to seven people who were faced with such problems as running a theater-ticket service, maintaining a suite of offices, and administering millions of dollars in funds. Its officers and directors were busily engaged in other activities.

The first Runyon Fund scrapbook I read covered the period of August-September 1953. The California drag race was held that September. Before then, someone had to come up with the idea for the race, enlist the necessary support, arrange for the publicity, and so on. Other people had to participate in the race and manage its running. Someone had to collect, count, and divide the receipts. A few weeks before the race, on August 3, there was a benefit baseball game for the Runyon Fund in California. It was before the major leagues moved west, and the competing teams were the Hollywood Stars and the Sacramento Solons. The pregame show included Groucho Marx, Jack Benny, Milton Berle, and Bob Hope. Between the benefit game and the drag race, the 1953 edition of Milton Berle's telethon took to the video waves, after someone had gathered up one thousand volunteers and disposed of the countless administrative details that plague such events. Edwin Powers of the Red Cross once gave me a rundown of what had to be done for his organization's flood-relief telethon—dozens of paid staff and volunteers spending days and nights full time for two weeks beforehand. I became completely exhausted just from listening. The same amount of effort was required for the Milton Berle extravaganzas.

While all this was going on, several civic groups in New Orleans were holding the Ugly Man Contest, for the benefit of the Damon Runyon Fund. Participants submitted a photograph apiece to attest to their alleged ugliness, and members of the public voted for the contestant of their choice. A penny had to be contributed to the Fund for each vote cast. The Fund's annual essay contest was in full swing during this time. A Los Angeles newspaper had just begun carrying a daily advertisement announcing that for every new subscription it would henceforth be sending a portion of the subscription price to the Fund. A Miami racetrack initiated a Damon Runyon Memorial Handicap, sending $5,000 of receipts to the Fund. In all these cases, there must have been people handling the administrative details that other charities form armies to deal with amid hoopla and slogans and poses of martyrdom. Maybe there were vaster armies behind the Damon Runyon Fund. If so, they were very quiet people.

Judging from his columns, Winchell himself was a pushover for the non-headliners who served his charity. On several occasions he referred to the kids in Harlem who performed a play in the basement of their tenement and charged a two-cent admission price, all proceeds (eleven dollars) going to the Runyon Fund. The children delivered the eleven hundred pennies to Winchell in four milk bottles. A few columns later, he mentioned the twenty-five dollars he had received from more-well-to-do youngsters from Warrenton, Virginia. They had raised the money by giving other children rides on their ponies. He repeatedly mentioned the Fraternal Order of Eagles. That organization made the Runyon Fund its special charity several years ago, and by now the Eagles have donated close to two million dollars to the Fund.

There seem to be several reasons for the Fund's devoted following. For one thing, it did nothing to attract enemies. It did not engage in a tug of war with other charities by launching massive direct-mail campaigns. It did not try to frighten or heart-tug the American public into contributing. It stayed away from the power politics that still goes on in the voluntary health field: petty disputes over whose directors will appear on a discussion panel, or whose medical advisory committee will be heard most intently by the National Institutes of Health, or whose executives will have their speeches most prominently displayed in the Congressional Record. At the same time, the Runyon Fund had a lot of glamorous friends who could and did give the charity a lot of free publicity. But it went deeper than that.

When Walter Winchell founded his organization, American charity was rapidly developing into the hollow, solemn, rather prissy world of business people, poseurs, and social elite that it is today. From the beginning, the Runyon Fund made itself known as a genuine character, a maverick that would rather attend a drag race or set up a bungalow on

Times Square than beat its breast in feigned agony or cite biblical quotations. It could accept $250 from Socks Lanza or $350,000 from the vending-machine industry without worrying about whether its image would be tarnished. And the house in which the Runyon Fund now resides is surely unique in the charity world. Somehow, I can't imagine any other charity existing under such a roof without half its membership resigning in outrage.

OLD NY SPEAKEASY BLDG. DONATED AS PERMANENT HQ FOR RUNYON FUND, said one of *Variety*'s more intelligible headlines, on November 6, 1963. Indeed, that elegant mansion on Fifty-sixth Street was once the famed Club Napoleon, run by the equally famed "Big Frenchy" De Mange. It had been no ordinary speakeasy. Dinner (plus) for four people could easily run five hundred dollars and more at Frenchy's prices. The house had been lavishly appointed in those days and very little had been unobtainable within its walls. It became so well known and admired that Hollywood selected it as the epitome of elegance in speakeasies and built a movie set just like it, down to the last detail. It was used to film *Night After Night,* in which George Raft had his first starring role and Mae West made the first of her many famous entrances—into the speakeasy, bedecked with jewels. "My goodness, what lovely jewelry," exclaimed the hat-check girl. West gave her the once-over and uttered these immortal lines: "Goodness, my dear, had nothing to do with it."

Come to think of it, the Runyon Fund shared several attributes with Mae West: a basic honesty, an earthy appeal, a disrespect for establishment venerations, and a very large sense of humor. Much of it had to do with the warm, zany, Runyonesque crowd that Walter Winchell attracted to his cause. But most of it had to do with Winchell himself. All the options were open to him. For example, he could have taken any of several uncandid approaches to his potential contributors. He rejected all of them. Instead, while other members of the voluntary health field were spending millions of hours and dollars to build great public dread and anguish for their various diseases, Winchell came right out in that first radio broadcast and referred to cancer as the "number two killer."

By the same token, Winchell undoubtedly had the power to limit Runyon Fund supporters to traditional fund-raising techniques. A lot of charm and spontaneity would have been lost, but there is no reason to believe that there would have been less money coming in. Nor was Winchell under any obligation to promise his public a 100 per cent return on charitable contributions. And even after he had made such a promise, he certainly could have voided it without much difficulty.

The path Winchell chose for the Damon Runyon Fund was dictated by a strong set of priorities. We came first— even before the cancer fight itself. As Dorothy Moore told me, it was a personal thing with him. And what he took most personally was our welfare. He didn't want us to worry whether our contributions were going where we intended. He didn't want to frighten, mislead, or annoy us. The idea was to give us an opportunity to contribute without disrupting our daily lives. If we wanted a theater ticket, we could buy one through the Fund and contribute to the cancer fight at the same time. We could choose a certain day to see a ball game or a drag race and help cancer research at the same time.

We contributors came away from Runyon fund raising with something extra. I don't mean an ident-o-tag. And I don't even mean a theater performance or a drag race or a play in a Harlem tenement. But rather, by participating in these events, we were actually *doing* something to help a worthy charitable cause, and we were doing it *together*. The people who attended only for the sake of sport or celebrity gazing may have had a good time. But they never experienced the most profound and enduring joy of all—the pleasure of being a charitable person, of joining with other good people in a selfless cause.

We have seen the *modus operandi* of other charitable organizations. Rather than encouraging us to rejoice in our own generosity, they force us to wallow in a variety of anguishes while asking for a contribution. Rather than treating us like intelligent human beings, they approach us through all the nit-witticisms of modern charity fund raising. Rather than providing us with an *opportunity* to contribute, they demand, badger, entrap, and even deceive us into giving. Their first priorities vary. For some, it is the cause. For others, it is a big contributor or a vocal membership or a prestigious board of directors. For a few, it is outright self-interest. But one thing is clear. In none of these cases do we —the contributors—come first. With Walter Winchell it was different.

He died on February 20, 1972. He had already lost most of his impact on America by then, as one of "his" newspapers after another folded. Milton Berle was no longer the giant of television entertainment. Many of the celebrities who had appeared on his telethons had died or entered retirement. New generations came to replace the people who had staged the Ugly Man Contest, the play in Harlem, and the drag race in California. The Damon Runyon Memorial Fund, like its namesake, lost its voice.

"We're called the quiet charity now," Dorothy Moore told me. She had joined the Fund sixteen years before as a volunteer and had "just stayed around," working her way up to the executive directorship. For a moment, her eyes seemed to stray back through those exciting years. She sighed. "We can't stay this way, of course. The administrative fund hasn't been making enough to cover even a quarter of our expenses. We've had to sell most of our securities, and we took a bad beating on the stock market in 1971."

At the end of fiscal 1968, the administrative-fund balance was $528,000. During that year, it had received over $300,000 in income, most of it coming from interest and dividends. Administrative expenses amounted to $156,000. By the end of fiscal 1972, the administrative-fund balance had dwindled to $144,700. Although administrative expenses rose only $14,000 during the five-year period—an incredible achievement, particularly in the charity world—administrative-fund income for fiscal 1972 was only about $39,000, slightly more than one tenth of what it had been five years before.

One of the saddest notes that appears on the Runyon Fund financial statements is the fact that contributions to the Fund have been steadily declining since 1968, while bequests from deceased benefactors have been steadily increasing. In fiscal 1968, the Fund received about $300,000 in contributions and slightly more than $600,000 in bequests. In fiscal 1972, it received less than $200,000 in contributions and $1.8 million in bequests. Because of the bequest income, the Runyon Fund was able to award $2.5 million in research and fellowship grants bringing the total to over $33 million in twenty-six years. But, considering that the theater-ticket-service income has remained about the same during the past five years, and that investment income has been nearly non-existent, and that the old crowd has been dying out, the picture is not at all bright.

At a board of directors meeting in October 1972, Walter Winchell's name was added to the Fund's title. There were several new directors present, and new plans to revitalize the Damon Runyon-Walter Winchell Cancer Fund were discussed. When I met with Dorothy Moore in May 1973, she told me that definite plans had yet to be finalized. But she said that their hope was to reconnect the Fund to the type of people who spoke for it during its heyday, to regain the zany charm that gave the charity its unique character. She said that certain things would never change. The Runyon-Winchell Fund would never charge its contributors one penny for fund raising or administration. Past contributors would continue to receive an annual report each year, unaccompanied by a solicitation letter. And the Fund's sole charitable purpose would remain cancer research.

I closed the scrapbooks and glanced out the window. Now the city was suffering evening rush hour. During the past twenty years, things had changed a bit out there as well. Amid all the soot and frenzy and out-of-order signs, was there still room for a bungalow on Times Square? And what about us? Time and again, we had been victimized and dehumanized by our charitable institutions, our national leaders, and our noble credos. Perhaps it was too late for all of us. But for Dorothy C. Moore, at least, that possibility did not seem to exist. Outside the office I was in, she finished rummaging through a file cabinet, closed the drawer, and switched off the lamp beside her. I stared at the lamp for a long time. I knew it wasn't lit. But, for some reason, it seemed to be burning very brightly.

10   Charity at the Brink

There are a lot of people in this country who are afflicted with epilepsy, a neurological disorder characterized by seizures produced by a surplus of electrical impulses from the brain. People do not die directly from epilepsy. But it is a truly horrible affliction—first, because loss of consciousness with little advance warning is a frightening experience and can indeed be fatal if you happen to be in the wrong place at the wrong time; second, because few other human conditions engender social reactions that are so deep, so emotional, and so adverse. At the hands of a misunderstanding society, epileptics have been treated with disdain, hatred, and disgust. They have been burned at the stake and ostracized from their fellow human beings. Although we have become more enlightened over time and although new drugs have been developed to control seizures in most of those afflicted, epileptics continue to bear painful and needless suffering in seeking a job, mingling socially with other people, and generally trying to lead fruitful lives.

Since it is not the type of condition one advertises, accurate statistics on the number of people afflicted are not available. Some estimates say two million Americans, others go as high as four million. But even if we use the lower figure, it means that there are twice as many epileptics in America as cancer patients under treatment; more people afflicted with epilepsy than with cerebral palsy, multiple sclerosis, muscular dystrophy, and tuberculosis combined. Epilepsy is a challenge for all of us—not only because its victims are so numerous, but also because we have all contributed to the difficulties of those victims by accepting, to some degree or other, the ridiculous myths that have made existence so painful for them.

The cause of this type of suffering is not epilepsy itself, but rather an unenlightened public that refuses to abandon notions of epileptics consorting with the Devil or being somehow cursed for committing unspeakable sins. There is an obvious antidote: public education. It has a familiar ring, of course. But only in terms of a health problem such as epilepsy can we realize that public education can indeed be a valid and needed program for a voluntary health charity. Elsewhere, we have seen too many abuses in this regard. The National Foundation of the 1940s and the American Cancer Society of the 1960s used their education programs to build public panics to their diseases, leaving the lingering question of whether more reasonable means could have been used to produce the worthy results that both organizations have achieved to date. And among today's health charities, we encounter public-education programs designed to reteach us the warning signs we already know backwards, to induce us to sympathize with the handicapped children we already love. The line between education and fund-raising promotion has become very thin indeed.

It is different with epilepsy. We can easily imagine a reasonable and intelligent public-education campaign that would effectively relieve epilepsy victims of the terrible social burdens they are now forced to bear. At the same time, despite the high incidence of epilepsy, the federal government has lumped the disorder together with several other neurological conditions and allocated only a minute portion of government research funds to the total. Conceivably, an educated and interested public would induce increased governmental concern. It has certainly happened before. Of course, waging such a campaign requires an effective organization which will serve as a rallying point, provide the necessary direction and leadership, and attract and dispense the funds needed to finance such an effort. Until now at least, the only type of organization that has arisen to meet such a challenge is the voluntary health charity. Moreover, what other type of organization is as capable of understanding the plight of epileptics, of fighting the laws that discriminate against them, of arranging for the counseling, employment, and other services to fill their needs?

The Epilepsy Foundation of America (EFA) claims to be the answer. It is, in fact, the only national voluntary health agency that represents those afflicted with epilepsy. And reading through the first few pages of its 1972 annual report, we find many reasons to believe that the EFA is capable of meeting the great challenges it has set for itself. There are, for example, several photographs of the charity's new national office in Washington—large, well appointed, filled with staff members who seem busily engaged in important activity. There are also photographs of research scientists, complicated-looking machines, celebrities, and EFA volunteers, all working through the organization for the cause of helping those afflicted with epilepsy. We learn that there are now 142 local EFA chapters throughout the nation, that Jack Lemmon is honorary national chairman, that the EFA board of directors is composed of forty-two people, mostly doctors and lawyers, that there is a large professional advisory board of medical people and a wonderful paid staff. With refreshing candor, the annual report starts out by admitting that the EFA does not have sufficient resources to deal with all the problems it should be solving. But it refers to the organization's tremendous growth, its many accomplishments, and its glowing future. The over-all picture presented through those first few pages is one of an effective national health charity, run by competent, straightforward executives and dedicated volunteers.

Midway through the annual report, the news from the EFA begins to deteriorate. On page twelve, for example, we learn that only fifty-one chapters have any paid personnel; that only fifty-six have bothered to appoint fund-raising chairmen. A few pages later, we are told the 142 chapters mentioned earlier are really only 106 chapters, the remainder being "in development." This revelation casts some large doubts on the report's earlier claims that EFA chapters offer epilepsy victims 170 counseling programs, 98 information and referral programs, and 438 public-education programs.

The 1972 financial statement begins on page twenty-three of the annual report. It says that the EFA raised $4.1 million that year at a fund-raising cost of $1.4 million, 34 per cent of total receipts. General management costs are re-

ported at $600,000, bringing supporting services to just un-
der half of total receipts for 1972. It seems extraordinarily
high for an established voluntary health agency. At the same
time, the EFA is relatively young; it was formed in 1967
through the merger of two smaller groups. And epilepsy is
certainly not the most salable cause on the charity market.
Furthermore, EFA fund raising seems to have improved a
bit. In 1971 the organization reported raising $3.4 million
and spending $1.2 million—35 per cent of receipts—on
fund raising, and $500,000 on management. If we believe
these figures, we must conclude that the EFA increased its
income by $700,000 during 1972, while its fund-raising
costs rose only $300,000. But there are reasons to question
the figures.

In the November-December (1972) issue of the EFA
newsletter, the organization's chief executive, Paul Funk,
predicted a 1972 fund-raising percentage of 39.8 per cent of
receipts. The very end of the year is a poor fund-raising
period, since people traditionally spend a great deal of their
earnings on Christmas gifts. It is highly unlikely that the
EFA fund-raising picture improved after Funk made his 40
per cent prediction. Furthermore, the EFA 1973 budget
sets expected fund-raising costs at 38.4 per cent of receipts.
It is highly unlikely that the EFA budgeted so much more
for fund raising in 1973 than it actually spent in 1972.

The organizational chart shows that publicity, public relations, media contacts, "celebrity recruitment," and similar matters are responsibilities of the EFA's information
and education department, which includes a deputy director,
four public-relations and media specialists, and clerks, and
typists. Their activities are not considered part of fund-raising costs. There is no way to tell how much time, if any,
these people devoted to fund-raising activities. All considered,

it seems reasonable to conclude that EFA fund-raising costs were at least a little understated for 1972.

We must certainly make some allowance for the fact that the EFA is not as well established as other organizations in the health field and for the public's unwillingness to recognize and support the epilepsy cause. But these are not the only factors behind the staggering fund-raising costs. In 1972, for example, the EFA spent over 10 per cent of its income—$419,755—on "fund-raising materials and supplies." One of the major reasons for this extraordinary expenditure is that in each solicitation letter it mails out, the EFA includes a bright new penny. It is a fund-raising gimmick of dubious propriety, and it costs the organization exactly one cent per letter, plus the cost of affixing the penny to the solicitation letter.

The EFA's use of fund-raising gimmicks seems traceable to one of its predecessor organizations, the Federal Association for Epilepsy (FAE). During the late 1950s, the FAE hired a fund-raising consultant named Harold Keats to conduct a direct-mail solicitation, mailing out a set of household labels with each solicitation letter. Fund-raising costs ran 60 per cent of receipts, most of it being paid to Keats and an Illinois mailing firm, the New Century Company. Ownership of New Century was vested in a man named Abraham Koolish (remember him?).

Former EFA employees told me that several people within the organization were opposed to use of the so-called "penny letter." Employees and volunteers have also been urging those who direct the organization to increase extra-campaign publicity and public education—not only to reduce future fund-raising costs, but also to forever quash the horrible myths that make life so miserable for those afflicted with epilepsy. For the most part, these objectives have not been achieved. And the primary reason has nothing to do with the age of the organization or the attractiveness of its cause.

The EFA's public-education program is the responsibility of the information and education department (I & E). In January 1972, the head of I & E was Don Organ. In April 1972, Organ was transferred from this position and made head of the chapter-services department. Around the same time, Joe Rizzo was hired to fill the post that Organ had vacated. The April 1972 issue of the EFA newsletter announced Rizzo's hiring and lauded him in glowing terms. In September 1972, Rizzo was transferred from I & E and made head of the fund-raising department.

In December 1972, Robert Jones was hired from a New York advertising firm to head the I & E fund-raising department. Les Blattner, a media specialist, was hired around the same time to serve as Jones's assistant. I spoke to them both on several occasions during April 1973. They struck me as competent people, experienced in media and publicity matters. They were enthusiastic. They said that their first priority was building up the EFA's puny public-education program. They had fresh, adventurous ideas they would soon put into effect. They told me that no one at the EFA had done an effective job of recruiting volunteer talent from Madison Avenue advertising firms and that they were on the verge of obtaining the free services of one of the top firms there. A week after I spoke to them for the last time, both Jones and Blattner had vanished from the EFA without explanation.

It is more than a little obvious that the EFA's public-education program could not be developed—or even conducted—with any effectiveness, so long as key I & E executives were mere EFA visitors, staying long enough to learn the ropes and pick up their paychecks before departing. Nor could intelligent policies be conceived and implemented under such circumstances.

During 1972, the EFA witnessed the departures of Michael Fought, a writer employed about three months; of Jean Worley, an office manager employed about four months; of Richard Hughes, an accountant who served less than six weeks. Two other accountants—Ronald Personett and Donald Kemon—resigned during the same year. Kemon was employed less than four months. The EFA's April 1972 newsletter announced that Sheldon Shalit, of the program-development office, would be turning out thirty-one new program guides for the organization. A few weeks after the announcement, Shalit was no longer associated with the EFA. During the same period, the EFA witnessed the comings and goings of several other employees.

"We used to joke about installing a turnstile at the front door," one of them told me. "And we started to call Rizzo's old office the ejection seat, because that's where most people wound up just before they disappeared. But it really wasn't so funny. Most of us wanted to do some good over there."

"You'd get in there in the morning and you couldn't be sure who would be back from the night before," said another former employee. "It was frightening. Someone would be working right next to you on Tuesday. And then . . . bam! Wednesday morning and just an empty desk. No explanation. Nothing. Just an empty desk, sitting there like a gravestone."

One of the most provocative items in the 1972 financial statement is also one of the smallest: $32,283 for "employment costs," mostly employment-agency fees. In Washington, employment agencies charge employers 10 per cent of a referred employee's first-year salary. This means that the EFA paid fees on a lot of first-year salaries during 1972.

It also means that the EFA was forced to hire too many people during 1972, five years after it started doing business.

The EFA's October 1972 newsletter contained a letter to the editor that accused the organization of inefficient management. In reply to this charge, the newsletter stated: "We strenuously disagree. So do our auditors, Price Waterhouse and Co. So does the management firm of Booz, Allen and Hamilton, which designed our management structure." But flinging out impressive-sounding names is hardly a defense to a very serious charge, substantiated in great part by the EFA's incredible employee turnover. In fact, an auditing firm does not comment on internal management, only on accounting practices. Price Waterhouse made this very clear in a letter published beside EFA financial statements in the 1972 annual report. By the same token, a management firm that sets up an organizational structure neither approves nor disapproves what occurs after its task is completed. Nor does it guarantee that its design will withstand the abuses of incompetent executives, high employee turnover, and such. And in the case of the EFA, the management design was altered dramatically after the Booz, Allen firm departed.

The initial organizational structure provided for an executive director at the top, a second rung of three deputy directors, and a third rung of six office chiefs. It was a good concept for an infant organization in that the first and third rungs could be filled in immediately. As activity increased and more co-ordination was needed, deputy directors could be hired later. Thomas Ennis, an attorney with several years of experience in non-profit organizations, was hired as executive director.

In December 1970 the EFA board of directors made a significant alteration in management structure by creating a new position above Ennis—executive vice-president—and hiring Paul Funk to fill it. It was a questionable decision.

For one thing, the EFA was a young organization and in desperate need of competent specialists at its lower executive levels—fund raisers, writers, program developers, publicists—people who would roll up their sleeves and make the contacts, build the chapters, and raise the money so essential to success in the initial stages. Rather than strengthening personnel at this level, the EFA made itself top-heavy with general administrators.

Furthermore, the EFA made a surprisingly large investment in order to obtain the services of its new executive vice-president. At the time, Ennis was being paid about $25,000 annually to serve as EFA chief executive. Funk's initial employment contract provided for an annual salary of $41,000 plus a bonus on signing of $12,000, almost twice what Ennis was being paid and certainly among the highest salaries in the charity world—and this from a charity with one of the lowest incomes in the health field. The National Easter Seal Society, for example, had an income of nearly $45 million in 1972—ten times that of the EFA—while paying its chief executive an annual salary of $36,000. Under his employment contract, Paul Funk is also entitled to the use of a leased automobile at EFA expense. In 1972, he chose a Buick Riviera; in 1973, a new AMX sports car at a cost to the EFA of $215 per month. In December 1972, Funk entered into a new employment contract, which provided for an annual salary of $44,500 plus a bonus on signing of $12,000.

In August 1973, I met with Arthur J. Grimes, membership director of the National Health Council, to discuss the activities of the Council and the value of Council membership as a guarantee of a charity's effectiveness and efficiency. It did not take us long to focus on the Council's newest member: the Epilepsy Foundation of America. Grimes told me that the Council had harbored serious doubts about admitting the EFA to membership, particularly because of its high fund-raising costs and use of the penny letter. But he said that Council concern over other phases of EFA operation had grown considerably during 1973. He mentioned the high rate of employee turnover and the number of highly paid executives.

"Do you know how much the EFA is paying its chief executive?" I asked him.

"Well, they've reported a starting salary of $44,000 a year," he said.

"Do you consider that out of line?"

"I'd say that was on the high side for an organization of that size. But not necessarily out of line."

"Suppose I told you that Funk's salary right now is $50,500?"

"I would say that was very high."

"Suppose I told you that Funk also gets the use of an AMX sports car at the organization's expense?"

"I would say that was extraordinary," Grimes told me.

Paul Funk, a former head of a large New York advertising firm, was a short, heavy-set man of Napoleonic bearing, he was volatile in temperament, brusque in personality, and large in ego.

He assumed absolute control of the EFA from the outset. Nothing was to be done without his approval. Not a word was to be spoken or written on behalf of the organization without having been first edited by his pen. "Maybe that kind of policy is okay when the organization is small and the chief executive efficient," said one former employee. "But Funk was incapable of doing anything on time. He'd let papers pile up for weeks, while we sat around and waited for his initials. The printing bills for the newsletter must have doubled, because the copy was so late all the time. And what made it all ten times worse was that he'd keep changing his mind. He'd finally approve Plan A, and when you tried to put it into effect, Funk would suddenly demand that you use Plan B."

He formed personal dislikes quickly and selected favorite targets for scapegoating. "He likes to whip people," a former employee told me. "I don't mean physically—but verbally. It's one of his kicks. Sometimes he'll get cute about it and, instead of letting you have it right out, set a long list of impossible things for you to accomplish. He'll keep reminding you about that list, watching you squirm. After a while, you just get fed up and walk out. I suppose that's why so many people have disappeared without a word."

Funk's antagonism did not extend to all EFA employees. In selected cases, he formed strong friendships and loyalties. And those who were so graced usually received substantial rewards as a result. Melba Gandy, for example, came to the EFA in early 1971, hired personally by Funk to serve as his secretary. She barely had time to acquaint herself with the secretarial ropes before she was given a promotion, a salary increase, and a new title: "Special Assistant to the Executive Vice President." In her new capacity, Gandy directed the EFA mail room and its employees. But this lasted only a few months. In March 1972, Melba Gandy was appointed deputy director in charge of government liaison and new-program development. Prior to her appointment, this was a third-rung organizational function. Whether the rearrangement was made for her benefit cannot be known. But it did result in considerably more prestige for Ms. Gandy and, according to the organizational chart, an annual salary of $25,000 as well. In less than two years, that was quite a large step for someone who had joined the organization as a secretary.

Other Funk favorites fared similarly during the same period. James Shannon was elevated from deputy director in charge of administration and finance to associate executive director. Robert Moore, who directed EFA administration while the organization experienced that incredible turnover in personnel, was promoted to fill Shannon's vacated slot. In a few months' time, a young man named Hugh Gage catapulted from directing EFA correspondence to head of I & E, another $25,000 position.

A kindergarten mentality gripped the EFA. The favored few and those who wished to join them constantly courted Funk's favor. The others stayed out of Funk's way, expending considerable energy trying to avoid the conflicts and unpleasantness he usually brought with him. Some of the Funk elite went so far as to spy on their fellow employees, carrying whispered reports back to their chief in hopes of winning further favored treatment. A secretary was called into his office to explain why she had thrown a particular scrap of paper into the wastebasket. Another secretary was confronted with a photograph Funk had taken of her desk top to prove she was messy.

Funk himself was seen on several occasions going through people's desk drawers after working hours. Employees began calling him "the Phantom." They were careful to lock their desk drawers before they left the office.

Funk demanded complete personal loyalty from his employees and complete personal service from his organization. He traveled extensively and, when he returned, he was not asked to substantiate his reimbursed expenditures. One of his former secretaries told me: "A few days after I started working there, he came back from a trip and told me to make out a voucher. I went into his office and asked him how much he had spent on the trip and on what. He wouldn't tell me. He just screamed and threw me out of the office. I knew that Melba Gandy had been his secretary before I came there. So I asked her what to do. She said that I should know who he was seeing and that I should just assume that he would be taking them out to lunch or dinner and picking up the tab. And I should make an estimate of what each dinner cost. From then on, I just made up the vouchers and he signed them."

There is, of course, no way to tell whether Funk was overcompensated for his travel expenses via the invented vouchers. Not even the secretary who invented the vouchers knew that. But, elsewhere, we find several reasons to believe that Paul Funk did not consider EFA economy a matter of top priority. There were those high salaries he paid out to the Funk favorites, for example. And there was his purchase of an expensive videotape machine and camera for the EFA. "I don't know what it's supposed to be used for," said one employee, "but I do know what it is used for. To build Paul Funk's ego. Every time he gives a speech, that camera is set up and turned on." None of the employees I interviewed could recall having seen the tapes used publicly, although some remembered seeing Funk himself watching himself on television.

Two EFA employees whom Funk hired in late 1972 told me that the major reason they accepted their new positions was that they were not making much money at their old jobs and Funk had given them offers they could not refuse. One of the two was Les Blattner, who walked out four months after he was hired. He told me afterward, "One time in my life I took a job because the money was good. I've never been more sorry about anything." The other employee was William Sutherland, a fund raiser hired as Joe Rizzo's assistant and promoted to deputy director for fund raising after Rizzo disappeared from the organization.[1] Sutherland

[1] By the way, after leaving the EFA, Rizzo was hired by another non-profit organization in a key executive position. As far as I can tell, all the people who left the EFA in dissatisfaction have found good jobs elsewhere.

had been in charge of fund raising at the Freedoms Foundation at Valley Forge, during periods when that organization
was incurring fund-raising costs of over 45 per cent of
receipts, nearly all the rest being eaten up by general administration.

Sutherland admitted to me that fund raising at the Freedoms Foundation had been a complete bust, and he blamed
the people in charge of the organization, not himself. He
said that the policy makers had refused to listen to his suggestions and that income had dwindled to a trickle as a result. "They hadn't paid my salary in three months," he told
me. "So I came here." As a deputy director, Sutherland fills
another $25,000 position.

It is entirely possible that the Freedoms Foundation's
fund-raising woes were not caused by Sutherland. He does
have fund-raising experience and he may be well qualified
for his job. According to the people I interviewed, however,
this is not the situation throughout the EFA, particularly at
its high echelons. "Most of the people getting those high
salaries aren't worth half of what Funk's paying them," one
former employee told me. "And they know it. That's how he
buys their loyalty. And even where that's not the case, it's
mostly an accident when a qualified person gets hired under
Funk's peculiar hiring policies."

Another former employee agrees: "If you're a woman,
the most important thing to him is how you look. I sent a
friend of mine to him for an interview and the first thing
Funk said when she walked through the door was: "Turn
around; I want to get a good look at you." With men it's
still a question of appearances. He wants them to have doc-
torates and master's degrees. He thinks it looks good for
public relations. But he doesn't want truly competent people. He's afraid they'll stand up to him, maybe even run to
Jack Anderson. So what does he get? A lot of shnooks with
letters after their names."

Hugh Gage may not fit both parts of that characterization. But he does have some letters after his name, attributable to a doctorate of philosophy he claims to have received from the University of Aberdeen in Scotland. Before his ascendancy to the head of I & E, Gage was lauded repeatedly by Funk in EFA newsletters and other literature. On each occasion, Funk referred to him as "Dr. Hugh Gage" or "Hugh Gage, Ph.D." Time and again, Funk claimed that Gage's awesome academic credentials qualified him to conduct various psychological and sociological studies for the EFA and, later, to head up the organization's public-education and communications enterprises.

When I interviewed him in April 1973, Hugh Gage was spending most of his time directing EFA correspondence, conducting research for the EFA on the side. With a minimum of humility, he told me about one of his surveys—a questionnaire to a cross section of people afflicted with epilepsy, which provided invaluable information to the EFA. The survey was directed at about eight hundred people—adult victims of epilepsy and parents of children who were afflicted with the disorder. All the people had been in previous contact with the EFA and had a deep interest in any effort aimed at gathering information on epilepsy problems. And yet, only 54 per cent of those contacted even bothered to reply. In a speech to an EFA conference, Hugh Gage stated: "The final returns were the highest in any survey I've ever been involved with."

The survey was seized as gospel by the EFA. In his conference speech, Gage emphasized the following point, underlined in the speech transcript: "Forty-six per cent of all persons reporting say they have been turned down for a job because of epilepsy, with factory, hospital and post office being the employer groups cited as offering the most problems in securing a job." Before these particular employers take offense, it should be noted that this conclusion was founded on the replies of only 216 people (parents of epileptic children were, of course, not asked to address the employment question). And of those 216 people, only 49 even bothered to address the employment question. And of those 49 people, only 46 per cent said they had been turned down for a job because of epilepsy. Finding a decent job is undoubtedly a serious problem for many people afflicted with epilepsy. But the experiences of a score of individuals across the nation hardly tell us whether, why, or how much in this regard. Nevertheless, Gage and the EFA have shown no hesitancy to treat such shaky data as irrefutable conclusions. Similar methods are employed in other phases of EFA activity.

The small EFA library is called the "information center" and praised throughout EFA literature as superlative. The display shelves of the information center contain long rows of EFA program guides, highly touted as providing all answers for chapters that want to build various types of comprehensive services for people afflicted with epilepsy. I studied three of the guides. None of them contained more than two thousand words of text. The most useful advice I obtained from any of them was the name of a government agency I might contact for information.

On page two of its annual report, the EFA stated: "The Foundation devoted $175,000 to research." The functional analysis of expenditures reveals that less than $90,000 of this amount actually went to the research scientists, the rest being eaten up by administrative expenses. In fact, the EFA spent over $50,000 in salaries to oversee less than $90,000 in research grants.

The 1972 annual report also lauded "several new basic studies on epilepsy and its ramifications, launched by the professional program staff in 1972." The studies I saw were produced by Melba Gandy's office and are indeed "basic," reading like high school term papers and containing little information of value, and no insights worth remembering.

On the chief executive's page of the 1972 annual report, Funk set out his future plans, emphasizing expansion of government-liaison, public-education, and patient-services programs. Once again, he stated: "To implement new plans we have an increasingly competent and well-trained group of headquarters Deputy Directors." Where? Expansion of the government-liaison program was the responsibility of Melba Gandy, who received most of her EFA training by typing invented travel vouchers and overseeing the EFA correspondence. Did this brief and very limited experience provide the best training for such a position? Of course not. But she was loyal to the chief executive and she shared his peculiar view of travel vouchers. Another mail-room graduate, Hugh Gage, would be developing the EFA's puny public-education program. What in Gage's background indicated that he would succeed where seasoned public-relations executives had failed? Not much. But he was not the sort to run to Jack Anderson, and he was lavish in his public praise of Paul Funk.

Why did it run so smoothly? There were forty-two people on the EFA board of directors during 1972. Many of them must have been intelligent people, sincerely interested in helping victims of epilepsy. And yet the evidence was right there under their noses. Employees were passing through the EFA as if it were a bus terminal. That seldom-used videotape machine was sitting smugly in the middle of the information center providing much more information on the nature of the EFA than its so-called program guides. High salaries and overnight promotions were being passed out to people of questionable merit for dubious reasons. There were many EFA employees who were outraged by these activities and who would certainly have related them to a concerned EFA board member. But they were not asked.

There seem to be several reasons for all of this. There are the facts, as we have noted, that the EFA is a relatively young organization and that its cause is not among the most popular in the charity world. As we have also seen, such excuses come too easily for charitable organizations and they can be used to hide some heinous management abuses. But when I first mentioned high fund-raising costs to EFA executives, these were indeed the justifications they hauled out. They seemed reasonable to me at the time, and an uninquisitive board member could easily accept such excuses and view all the symptoms of mismanagement as growing pains, without looking further.

When the EFA was formed, in 1967, there were several strong local epilepsy groups already in existence, which later became EFA chapters. These groups continued to function on their own—quite apart from what was going on in Washington—developing new programs and obtaining government grants, with little assistance from the Funk regime. Paul Funk could and did hold out their accomplishments as EFA accomplishments, thus camouflaging the meagerness of national-headquarters successes.

According to the EFA staff manual, the chief executive officer is the only liaison between the board of directors and the paid staff. It was, therefore, Paul Funk who provided the board members with information on national-headquarters activity, together with his own characterization and justification of what was happening. When you control the news, you can get away with telling only a small part of the story, hoping that people will accept what you give them without question. So it seems to have been at the EFA. During an interview with a key board member, I asked for his views on the EFA's high fund-raising and management costs. "You must be kidding," he said smiling. "Our fund-raising costs are below 30 per cent." I suggested he look at an annual report which he did. "Hmmmm," he said.

The size of the board of directors is misleading. The list of 1972 committee assignments for board members reveals that seven people—members of the executive committee and vice-presidents of the Foundation—held a disproportionate share of chairmanships and key committee positions. According to former employees, they formed a closely knit power nucleus on the EFA board. They were the people who awarded Paul Funk a sports car and a $50,500 annual salary, indicating a certain lack of interest in the careful use of other people's money. Some of them were active participants in the Federal Association for Epilepsy during that organization's association with the Keats-Koolish fund-raising team. All of this indicates a very great lack of interest in the careful use of other people's money.

At a staff meeting held in early 1973, Paul Funk announced with satisfaction that his design for the EFA, particularly national headquarters, had neared completion. He had reason to be pleased. Through careful testing and selection, he had developed a hard-core group of Funk loyalists, gradually elevating them to key staff positions, further insuring their loyalty with salaries they probably could not attract in a saner environment. All the employees I interviewed, some still working for the EFA at the time, told me that Thomas Ennis was the most reliable key executive on the staff. In a short three years, Funk and the board of directors had worked in concert to demote Ennis from head of the EFA to second in command of the EFA and then, according to minutes of the staff meeting, to one of Funk's two "executive assistants," responsible mainly for forward planning. "They should not have to concern themselves with the day-to-day problems of the Foundation," the minutes say.

"Ennis is Funk's biggest problem," said a former employee. "He's too popular to fire and too honest to trust. The Funk plan is to put him on a shelf somewhere—keep him traveling around the country and drawing up plans for 1980."

As of the summer of 1973, the future of the EFA does not seem at all sunny. There are undoubtedly people who care sprinkled liberally throughout the organization. But they are disconnected and uninformed. There is no reason to expect a dramatic change, now that Funk has solidified his control of the organization and weeded out most of the upstarts. What seems much more likely is that the EFA will settle into a well-oiled machine geared to executive self-interest and mutual back-scratching and fueled by easy money, false appearances, and lack of accountability. The outward signs of abuse will disappear as the EFA becomes more adept at disguising fund-raising costs and selecting the right kind of employees. The Epilepsy Foundation of America will become one of the most respected charities in America. And the Thomas Ennises, the concerned board members, the dedicated volunteers, the people afflicted with epilepsy, the contributors who want to help them—we will all be forgotten. Unless, of course, we do something about it.[2]

[2] See chapter 15.

11   Charity with a Bonus

I am holding a typical issue of a typical family magazine, reading one of those typical cutesy articles on the letters children write to the adult world. One of the letters says: "I make Christmas cards and sell them. I give the money to you for people who are starving and dying. It makes you feel good that you are saving someones life out there in that great big world of ours. I will do this as long as I live and teach my children to do this and give to CARE." The same article relates the tale of a little girl who sent a nickel to Richard Nixon "for the poor people," which Nixon forwarded to CARE. The nickel was used to buy two bricks for a house built recently in Bangladesh. HER 5¢ BOUGHT TWO BRICKS, the headline reads.

It is all very typical, of course. Aside from children, the Lennon Sisters and Richard Nixon, CARE has certainly been the star attraction of the family-magazine circuit. The articles are always sloppy in praise and human interest, usually written with such gushing sweetness that you know it has to be a pack of lies. Well, it isn't. In fact, CARE's proclivity for saccharine publicity is just about its only weakness. And those syrupy tones are so contrary to the organization's true nature that we can easily dismiss even this lonely charge against it.

CARE is a lean, hard-nosed, efficient organization. It maintains sixteen field offices in the United States and Canada and a national office in New York City, through which it annually raises $11.1 million in contributions and nearly $8 million in government grants and other income; purchases $10 million in food and equipment for overseas shipment; receives $69 million in government-surplus foodstuffs for overseas distribution; and arranges for the packaging and shipping of all food and equipment—nearly $100 million worth—to overseas destinations. Fund raising and general management run $3.1 million—28 per cent of cash contributions, 16 per cent of total income, and if we include the value of commodities distributed, an incredible 3 per cent of program services. If you made a contribution to CARE in 1972, each dollar you donated produced nearly ten dollars' worth of overseas services.

One reason for this remarkable charity value is Public Law 480, a federal statute that enables private organizations providing overseas assistance to obtain free agricultural commodities from the United States Government. The commodities are surpluses that the government buys to assist farmers.

The statute also provides for payment of overseas shipping costs on PL 480 commodities by the federal government. During 1971 the government provided over $139 million in agricultural commodities to foreign-aid charities and paid out over $44 million in shipping costs, with CARE receiving about 40 per cent of each.

Although there are more than eighty charities that assist people overseas, the lion's share of PL 480 commodities are distributed by CARE, Catholic Relief Services, and Church World Service. Some of the other foreign-aid charities have developed their programs in different directions and do not have the capability of delivering large quantities of foodstuffs. Others seem to be deliberately avoiding all contact with the government, presumably under force of the "government-aid-leads-to-government-control" theory of charity management. "That's nonsense," Frank Goffio, CARE's executive director, told me. "If you're doing what you want to do without compromising your principles, you're not prostituting yourself by taking money from the government and you're not being controlled by anyone. Look us over and let me know if you think we've compromised on anything." Actually, in nearly thirty years of existence, CARE has demonstrated a remarkable amount of principle, dedication, and determination in carrying out its mission.

Its full name—Cooperative for American Relief Everywhere—is traceable to the organization's birth, in late 1945. It was formed by twenty-two existing organizations—many of them religiously oriented—as a co-operative distributing agency of voluntary aid to war-torn Europe. As originally conceived, CARE's role was limited to designated relief: food packages for individuals, rather than general assistance to communities and nations. The first shipment of CARE packages arrived in Le Havre, France, on May 11, 1946.

During the following few years, many of the agencies involved in the organization came to believe that individual aid was not enough, that CARE should expand its programs to include other types of assistance. Several of the biggest religious organizations disagreed vehemently. But their representatives were a minority on the CARE board. The smaller agencies refused to compromise and the larger groups split off and founded independent foreign-aid charities.

In 1950, CARE initiated its first self-help programs by providing agricultural equipment to farmers overseas. In 1951, PL 480 was passed, enabling CARE to expand its food packages to large quantities of commodities. In 1962, CARE brought another organization into its fold: MEDICO, founded by Dr. Thomas A. Dooley four years earlier and dedicated to bringing medical talent and supplies to underprivileged nations. And in 1967, CARE established a new type of self-help program, in which it joined in partnership with a foreign government to assist the government in a specific shared-cost construction project. The first such project was a school to be constructed in Honduras. Throughout its history, CARE demonstrated a remarkable flexibility in adopting new programs to suit changing times and needs—a very rare quality for a large organization, particularly a charity. At the same time, the essential principles upon which CARE was founded remained unaltered. They are very much in evidence today.

Unlike too many charities in the foreign-aid field, CARE issues annual financial statements, which are available upon request to any member of the public. And unlike nearly every charitable organization in America, giving to CARE does not mean that your name will thence be passed from one charity to another. "We've never rented our list to anyone and we've never exchanged our list with anyone," Frank Goffio told me, "and we never will." It may seem an

insignificant matter. But we are talking about a very productive mailing list of several million people, which means
"$50 per M" on the open market for each rental, which adds
up to a lot of dollars that CARE is giving up just so its contributors will not be annoyed. Most important of all, Frank
Goffio is proud of it!

By visiting any of its offices, you can find other aspects of
CARE that have remained unaltered from the beginning.
CARE national headquarters is located in a former brewery
on First Avenue in New York. "It's the cheapest office
space in the city," Goffio told me, again with considerable
pride. And there is every reason to believe him. The elevator
is an ancient relic that groans with each breath-taking inch
of progress. The walls are in desperate need of new paint,
the floors in desperate need of new floors. The only frill I
could detect was a moth-eaten carpet in one of the closetlike
offices. The CARE Washington office is located in one of the
oldest office buildings in the city. It is a suite of minuscule
dimensions, furnished with scarred desks and metal cabinets.
I recognized only one room from past travels through the
charity world—the storage closet. But even this was different.
The shelves should have been piled high with lavishly produced brochures and manuals and pamphlets, mostly dupli-
cates of other brochures, manuals, and pamphlets. But here
there was only a stingy supply of material, all turned out on
cheap paper, with few photographs and very little color.
If CARE was spending our money on anything but bare
essentials, it was doing a very good job of hiding the extravagance.

The most impressive thing about the two CARE offices I
visited was the nature of the people in them. To a person,
they struck me as a very determined group—idealistic and
compassionate, yes; but also remarkably realistic. Theirs is
the type of approach reflected in a dinner speech given by

Dr. Peter D. Comanduras, who joined with Tom Dooley to found MEDICO in 1958: "Let me give you a capsule distillation of world conditions as they really are. Of the two hundred human beings born every minute, one hundred sixty will be colored—black, red, yellow, or brown. About half of those will be dead before they're a year old. Of those that survive, half will be dead before they reach the age of sixteen. The survivors will have a life expectancy of thirty years. During this brief and wretched existence, they will be sick and hungry most of the time. Most of them will never learn to read or write. Their homes are tents and mud huts. Others have no shelter. They lie seminaked in the alleys and byways of Asia, Africa, and Latin America. Waiting. Hoping. Starving."

The CARE people are proud of the organization they work for. "I suppose the thing I like best about CARE is that we don't degrade people by just handing out alms," I was told by Suzanne Wright, assistant director of the Washington office. "If people are in a crisis situation, if they're unable to produce enough food or cope with a natural disaster, then we give emergency relief with no strings attached. But they just can't sit back and live off CARE and our contributors. They have to work with us, develop their own capabilities so that we can go out of business in that country and move on to another one."

CARE does not solicit customers. Before CARE can provide assistance, the foreign government must request its help. What usually happens is that the people in a nation that neighbors on one in which CARE is already at work will look over their border, realize the value of CARE assistance, and request it. CARE will then explain to the new government's leaders that several things must happen before it will agree to enter the country: The government must agree to allow entry of CARE commodities duty-free, to help arrange and pay for inland transportation of those goods, and to protect CARE against legal suits and entanglements while operating in the country. CARE must also conduct a survey within the country in which it analyzes whether the country has true needs that CARE can meet and whether the country and its citizens are sincerely ready to join with CARE in self-help programs. Finally, CARE and the foreign government must sign a "Basic Agreement," which clearly defines the relationship between them. After the Basic Agreement is signed, CARE will establish a mission in the country, comprising a mission chief and a small staff.

The first responsibilities of the mission are to conduct an in-depth survey of specific needs, to develop proposals for particular projects and to work with the foreign government to devise a long-range plan. The latter will include numerous projects, each timed and budgeted. The plan will be designed to attack a broad range of problems—nutritional educational, economic. For each project, the foreign government or one of its local communities will provide labor and as much money as possible. CARE will provide equipment, expertise and money where required.

Frank Goffio told me: "We're constantly trying to avoid several pitfalls that we've seen in other agencies and even fallen into ourselves. They all involve the same human weakness: shortsightedness. It's easy to just give food to a hungry person and leave it at that. But that doesn't really solve that person's ignorance about nutrition. And if something happened to our food shipments, that person would starve to death. The same type of problem arises in construction of physical plants. A country sees one of its neighbors building a school with our help. So it wants a school. But that school isn't going to solve anything by itself." CARE guards against the danger of an empty schoolhouse in two ways: first, by devising a long-range plan in advance that provides for complete and comprehensive programs, not just one-shot projects; second, by maintaining a CARE mission in the country to make sure the programs work.

As of this writing, CARE has 150 employees serving in thirty-four countries. Their accomplishments are mind-boggling. During 1972, they helped feed 28 million people, mostly children—14 million people in India alone. They supervised construction of 504 primary schools, 17 secondary schools, and 97 nutrition centers that will feed 150,000 children. They helped build safe-water sources for 339 communities. They provided counsel and equipment to 562,400 farmers. But their contribution to such continuing programs is only part of the service provided by CARE personnel overseas. They are in continuous friendly contact with both the citizens and government officials of the country in which they are stationed. They often serve as informal arbiters, advisers, and liaison people—greasing wheels, soothing ill feelings, and finding simple solutions to complex problems. A former mission chief told me: "A few years ago in Hong Kong the community leaders and government officials were having a terrible time getting the nutritional program off the ground. There was a lot of bickering. The mothers weren't showing much interest. So I suggested that they form the Hong Kong Infant Feeding Society. It worked beautifully. They forgot their differences and launched a fantastic campaign to educate mothers and feed babies. I'll never forget it."

Combined with CARE's awesome resources, the cordial relationship of CARE personnel with government officials produced quick and effective responses to two terrible 1972 disasters. Within moments of the December earthquake that struck Managua, Nicaragua, CARE director James Puccetti was conferring with Nicaragua officials, arranging for CARE emergency relief. Arrangements were quickly finalized and, a few hours later, CARE commodities were being flown in from stockpiles in Costa Rica and Honduras. During the summer of 1972, CARE officials in devastated Bangladesh somehow managed to cut through the governmental chaos of the new nation, finalize arrangements for an emergency housing-relief program for 34,000 refugees, and supervise construction of 5,639 brick houses.

There is no great mystery surrounding these achievements. CARE employees are certainly not super-beings, although they must be terribly dedicated and talented. If they accomplish more than equally dedicated people working for other groups, it is because of the reputation and efficiency of the organization behind them. And these qualities are traceable to several factors. For one thing, CARE has an edge in experience, being the first to enter the voluntary-foreign-aid and self-help fields. As a result of its early presence in postwar Europe, it received considerably more publicity and dramatic news coverage than other organizations of its type. In attracting the right type of personnel, all overseas charities have an advantage over domestic organizations, particularly now that voluntary foreign aid to Europe has been redirected to underprivileged nations. These are not soft jobs. Executives who seek expense accounts and sports cars will seldom turn to a foreign-aid charity. Those who do are usually very special types of people. And for the past twenty years or so, CARE and its fellow overseas charities have had the benefits of PL 480, certainly an extraordinary bonus. All these things were certainly crucial to CARE's success, but they don't tell the full story.

Throughout its history, CARE has shown an extraordinary commitment to serving only the needy—and the most needy, if possible. When Europe got back on its feet, CARE packed up and got out. It could have stayed much longer. When assistance to individuals proved ineffective in meeting the challenges posed by underdeveloped nations, CARE abandoned this approach. It could have continued to hand out food packages. CARE's insistence on seeking out those who needed it the *most* brought a bonus. Where there is great deprivation, even a very little money and effort can result in dramatic improvement overnight. In 1961, for example, CARE took an $875 donation from employees of an insurance company and used it to buy 1,400 fruit trees for a group of families living on Guatemala's Pacific coast. The people were living in crude shacks, subsisting on a meager diet. There were no jobs, no hope of improvement. CARE gave each family an average of thirty-five trees and advice on how to grow them. In four years, the 1,400 trees had become, through graftings, 134,000 trees. Two years later, the number of trees had risen to 255,000. By 1966, there were four hundred orchards where none had been five years before. The people began marketing their produce, using the proceeds to build solid homes, acquire proper food for their families, and educate their children.

Such is the stuff of which human-interest stories are made. And human-interest stories mean free publicity and more donations. But it goes much deeper than that. Dramatic results provide strong inspiration for an organization's employees, making up for the low salaries, tiny offices, and other anguishes imposed upon those who work for a penny-pinching enterprise. And dramatic results make it much easier to work with potentially hostile charity recipients, bureaucrats, and government leaders. So it has been with CARE.

Where, then, did CARE acquire its commitment to the needy, its dedication to economy, its concern for its contributors, and its remarkable blend of flexibility and uncompromising principle? Where did it all come from? From wherever the power is, of course. And the power to control

CARE's destiny is vested in a board of directors composed of representatives from each of CARE's member agencies, most of them groups that helped organize the co-operative in 1945. The board encompasses a broad spectrum of organizations, including the General Federation of Women's Clubs, the National Farmers Union, the Fraternal Order of Eagles (also big supporters of the Damon Runyon-Walter Winchell Cancer Fund, see chapter 9), the National Council of Negro Women, United HIAS Service, the National Grange, and the Salvation Army. They demonstrated their principled stubbornness by refusing to bow to the big religious organizations on the question of designated relief. And the many remarkable qualities of the organization they direct stand as convincing evidence of their deep appreciation of charity.

It seems an appropriate note on which to end our brief tour of American charity. Looking back from the height of CARE, we can see too many organizations that suffer badly in comparison. There are many reasons. But the primary ones certainly lie at the centers of power. Too many of our charitable organizations are controlled by too few people. They have erected too many barriers between us and the needy people we are eager to help: barriers such as self-interest (and lack of interest), petty quarrels, bureaucratic waste, arrogance, deceit.

CARE is showing us a better way. It is telling us that charity does not mean an American flag, a celebrity parade, a heartbeat, or a fancy brochure. Rather, it means needy people on one side, generous people on the other side, and a lot of dedication, compassion, sacrifice, and hard work in the middle.

Part 4

A Contributor's Guide

Two things are undeniable: First, many of our charities are wasteful; others are ineffective; some are even fraudulent. Second, there is no way to determine with absolute certainty whether a particular charity will make the best possible use of our money. This should not be the case. We should not be subjected to any risk at all in making a charitable donation. But we are.

Charity executives believe that once we recognize these unpleasant truths, we contributors will become much less generous, perhaps even turn away from charity altogether.

They may be right. If we accord top priority to riskless giving, we have no alternative. Only by closing our check-books completely can we obtain absolute protection against being suckered out of a donation or being victimized by an imperfect charity organization. Furthermore, after being kicked around all these years, there would be a certain emotional gratification in responding to the next charity appeal with an old-fashioned thumb to the nose. But there are good reasons for resisting such a temptation.

Avoidance has too often proved a self-defeating method of protection against imperfect social systems. Voters who stay away from the polls because they are fed up with crooked politicians have, through non-involvement, helped elect a lot of crooked politicians to office. Similar things could happen to American charity if the most aware con-tributors were to turn away in disenchantment. The frauds would have a field day while worthwhile organizations folded because they refused to exploit the naïve. It is perhaps difficult to believe that the amount of our individual contributions would have any impact at all on so vast an enterprise as American charity. But we are much more in-fluential as individuals than we think, and many of our most worthwhile charities are subsisting on starvation diets. Our non-support could well prove fatal for those organiza-tions. And if only the promoters and entrenched organiza-tions were to survive, American charity would become a rather meaningless enterprise.

As matters now stand, our charity system is certainly far from ideal. But in deciding whether to deny it our support, we must ask whether we want to contribute to its downfall. The possibility may seem remote. But it is far too grave to ignore. We must also consider what American charity can ideally become. Social systems do change, sometimes for the better. If we decrease or deny funds to all charities, we are punishing the worthwhile organization and the dedicated charity executive along with the rest, depriving them of adequate means to influence positively the *status quo*. Finally, we cannot forget the realities of our modern world. If we want to be charitable, we need a charity system that can receive and make effective use of our donations. It is, therefore, the phenomenon of charity itself that must be weighed against the risks involved in giving.

One of the traditional arguments in favor of charity has been weakened considerably by governmental activity in social-welfare areas. When it comes to helping needy people, no charitable organization on earth can hope to match the massive programs of our federal government that aid the poor, the hungry, and the homeless both here and abroad. Indeed, there is no area of charitable endeavor that has not been taken up by the government, overshadowing the work of private organizations with its staggering resources. If we look only at the numbers, it is difficult to conceive of anything now provided by charities that could not be provided by government ten times over. Of course, this is only a small part of the charity transaction.

From a contributor's point of view, government welfare, health-research, and foreign-aid programs are as distant from charity as is General Motors. For us, charity entails a certain personal involvement with a cause and the freedom to give or not to give. Neither element is present in our support of government welfare programs. We are required to send in a check under penalty of fine and imprisonment. We don't know how most of the money is spent. Since we have no choice in the matter, there seems little point in finding out. Newspapers provide us with plenty of reasons to believe that a lot of our tax money is being wasted. And it is difficult to take pleasure in our support of government cancer research while we are being so brutally treated by inequitable tax laws and various government misspendings. When government takes money from us, the most pleasure it can give us is the vague feeling that we are being good citizens. Charity offers us the very real opportunity of being good people.

It is not something to be taken lightly. We are, after all, what we do to other people. The complexities and depersonalizations of modern life have disconnected us from the needy, from the people and problems that require our attention, from ways to be helpful and human. I can conceive of no better remedy for this critical problem than an effective charity system which channels freely given donations to worthwhile purposes and also gives us the opportunity to participate personally with volunteer time. No matter how vast the government welfare system becomes, it will never meet this great challenge.

It also seems rather apparent that government is neither very adventurous nor very flexible in dealing with critical social needs. It usually takes heavy and repeated proddings to interest our public officials in a new welfare program, and similar action to force a change of direction once the ball is lumbering on its way. Charitable organizations have proved effective in dealing with this problem. The American Cancer Society and the American Heart Association deserve much of the credit for the huge government research programs for their particular diseases. That government interest in neurological diseases has been minimal until now is due at least in part to the dearth of effective charity organizations in this area. A reorganized and revitalized Epilepsy Foundation of America would certainly be able to mobilize public support for increased government research into neurological health problems.

I could spend the next fifty pages and more relating the numerous past accomplishments of American charity—the cures for many diseases, the disaster victims assisted, the hospital bills paid. Indeed, this is the type of argument set forth by most of the charity executives I interviewed when I pointed out all the risks involved in giving. I do not believe that it is wise to follow their example. For one thing, accepting such an argument requires giving some credence to the end-justifies-means approach that has produced so many evils in the charity world. That a particular charity organization has supported a successful or worthwhile project with some of our money does not automatically erase the fact of its misuse of other funds or its deceitful fund-raising practices. Furthermore, the past triumphs of American charity do not really provide us with much enlightenment regarding the problem of charity evaluation. It does not tell us whether the organizations that produced those achievements should have accomplished more with the resources they had, or whether today's charities will do as much good tomorrow.

Finally, and most important, to dwell on all those past accomplishments means treating charity as more of a commodity and less of an idea. As a commodity, the value of charity to society is a complex matter varying with time and circumstance, raising such questions as the incidence of a particular disease, the extent of government activity in the welfare field, and perhaps even the nature of public opinion on certain social issues. But as an idea, charity remains an unvarying essential for a people's faith in itself, for human pride and principle and purpose. We must maintain charity as a viable concept. There is no alternative. Once we accept this, and recognize the fact that charity cannot exist without a system to support it, we must reject the possibility of denying or decreasing our donations of time and money to that system.

The situation is not unlike the one we encounter every day in the marketplace. We know that there are frauds and exploiters throughout our business system, waiting to victimize us when our automobile breaks down or our food supply runs out. Nevertheless, we still get our transmission repaired and return to the supermarket, hoping that we will have the wisdom to effectively protect ourselves. We have no choice in the matter. We must subject ourselves to the risks in order to survive. Our survival as human beings, as members of society, requires that we be generous to American charity, no matter what the risks we may be facing as contributors.

This does not mean that we are forced to contribute in total blindness, with only a prayer for protection. There are ways to minimize the risks involved in being charitable.

13   Give Carefully!

In seeking to protect ourselves as contributors, our first concern must be for the outright charity promoters. They are the people who deliberately set out to deceive us, to exploit our benevolent instincts to their personal advantage. With their enterprises, the danger is not merely that some of our money may be diverted to non-charitable purposes, but that every penny we contribute will wind up in the promoters' pockets.

The Warning Signs

Every charity appeal, legitimate and otherwise, is designed to touch some emotional chord. Worthwhile charities may use some questionable techniques to accomplish this, but they are always directed at our positive emotions: kindness, sympathy, love, benevolence. Charity promoters often appeal to our negative instincts as well. We are asked to help veterans and defend the nation against long-haired radicals; to assist poor people in Appalachia rather than welfare cheats in Harlem. Causes that seem designed to make people angry or afraid should be regarded with considerable suspicion. And if the cause relates to a recent event—flood, mine disaster, political development—it may well have been concocted for exploitation purposes alone. It takes a lot of money to launch a charity solicitation, and wealthy benefactors usually work through established, well-known charities. A citizens' drive to help flood victims will usually publish a long list of sponsors with its charity advertisement.

Established charities almost never use telephone solicitors. If you are telephoned by someone who purports to be representing a struggling local group, that person may be sincere and the cause worthwhile. But there is reason to be careful. The same is true of the shabbily dressed child who appears at your door with a box of candy.

A favorite technique of charity promoters is to name their phony groups after worthwhile charities, hoping to confuse us into making a donation. Charities do not change their names overnight. If there is an "American" where a "National" used to be, watch out!

Worthwhile charities do not keep their accomplishments secret while asking for donations. As we have seen, quite the contrary is true. If the solicitation letter you receive contains only rhetoric without indicating how many children the charity has been feeding or how many research grants it has been making, there is a good chance the letter was authored by a charity promoter who is clever enough to avoid telling an outright lie and thereby commit mail fraud.

The Initial Defense

The most effective weapon in a charity promoter's arsenal is our blind emotion. Our best defense against such a weapon is self-restraint. I do not suggest that we desensitize our giving. Meaningful charity cannot be reduced to the level of a business transaction. We should indeed have compassion for the child we are trying to feed; we should be concerned about the disease we are trying to cure. Otherwise, there is no personal involvement, no pleasure or sense of purpose in giving. But when one of the warning signs appears, or when there is other good reason to doubt the validity of the charity appeal, we hardly serve the cause of charity by rushing to our checkbook. We only help further the very uncharitable work of the promoters and exploiters.

Resisting the pitch of a charity promoter is not always easy. These are people who have spent years learning practical human psychology. They know us better than we know ourselves, and they direct their appeals to our most vulnerable emotional areas. They have been aided in their work by our most reputable charities, organizations that have built their successes on public panic, celebrity endorsements, and similar methods of producing reflexive contributor reaction. One charity executive has developed a mental tool that he claims works well in helping to resist the most effective charity pitch. "A couple of years ago, I imposed a mandatory period on myself. I wait at least a week before I take any action on a charitable solicitation, no matter where it comes from or how good it sounds. It gives me time to think, and it also gives me a good excuse for the nice person who comes to the door and asks for a donation."

A reputable charity will certainly be around a week later to accept your money. There is no reason to rush. There are a lot of reasons to be careful.

The Minimal Inquiry

When you are solicited in person or by telephone, you have been presented with an opportunity to conduct a simple and effective test. The fact of the matter is that charity promoters do not like to answer questions. They thrive on their own anonymity and on the naïveté of their victims. Ask a few questions and wait for a reaction. There is no need to be aggressive about it. You might frighten the well-meaning volunteer who is working for a deserving local group. Just a few amiable questions about the name of the person doing the solicitating, his or her connection to the organization, who else is involved in the charity. Names. Addresses. Telephone numbers. Those are the type of questions that frighten or anger the promoter. And if the solicitor does become frightened, angry, or evasive, your interest in the cause should become considerably less compelling.

Most charity promoters conduct their solicitations by mail. In such a situation, a direct inquiry is not possible. But that does not mean that you should decide whether to contribute without making any inquiry at all. Each year, an inestimable number of American contributors give away an inestimable number of hard-earned dollars to fraudulent charity appeals without making the slightest effort to determine whether the appeals are run by viable charitable organizations. It is a simple matter to determine. All you have to do is request an annual report and as much information as possible on the organization's activities. This can be done either by letter or by telephone. As was my experience in seeking information from foreign-aid charities, there are some organizations that will not provide you with an annual report. But in almost every one of these cases, they will send you newspaper clippings, names of some of their well-known supporters, and similar information that shows there is an organization back there, not just a charity promoter and a mailing list. If this information is not sent to you, further investigation should be conducted before you send in a contribution.

These are minimal measures, of course. They do not carry with them a foolproof guarantee that you will never again be victimized by a fraudulent or worthless charity. But they do offer considerable protection against the great majority of fly-by-night charity promotions, and they do not entail very much time or effort—just a wary eye, a few questions, and a ten-cent stamp. Of course, even writing a short letter can seem like a lot of trouble when you're in a lazy mood and the cause seems all right and you're only planning to send in twenty-five bucks anyway.

When you start feeling that way again, you might consider three things: First, once you fall for an outright charity promotion, you have made the golden sucker list. Your name will be passed from one direct-mail entrepreneur to another. You will become a target. The odds of the next charity appeal you receive being a phony will skyrocket. How does that strike you? Second, behind every charity-for-profit there is an individual who takes great delight in deceiving innocent people like you. A few days after you send in your twenty-five-dollar check, that person will run over to the bank and cash it. Maybe he'll put the money toward a Bahamas vacation or maybe he'll just blow it all on dinner at a plush restaurant. Think of him basking in the sun or sipping Mouton-Rothschild at your expense. Not a very pleasant picture, is it? Finally, one day you may just read in the newspaper that a charity you have been carelessly supporting is a phony. You will be angry, frustrated, embarrassed. You may well seek revenge against charity in general, turning your back on worthwhile organizations that desperately need your help. You may convince your friends to react in the same manner. And we will all be in terrible trouble. Now, do you request that annual report?

14   Give Wisely!

Although the outright promoters certainly commit the most outrageous charity abuses, it is relatively easy for a contributor to obtain a maximum of protection against such people with a minimum of effort. This is because such promoters usually solicit contributions through empty shells that will not stand up against even the most basic inquiry. All that is needed is a little care and restraint. The promoters will usually tip their hand before it becomes necessary to conduct an in-depth study.

Detecting the various abuses of viable charity organizations—including their occasional arrangements with people like Abraham Koolish—is a much more difficult task. The only sensible way is to obtain as much information as possible on each charity that interests us and then to make an objective evaluation of that organization's worth. There are several obstacles along the way. As we have seen, charities are generally unwilling to disclose intimate details about their operations to contributors. And the information we can obtain has been filtered through the organization and often distorted to serve the ends of the people who control it. Furthermore, there are so many variables and puzzlements involved in fund raising and other aspects of charity management that universal standards by which to judge a charity are very difficult to establish. Finally, evaluating a charity requires a certain amount of subjective judgment that must be left to the individual. You and I might disagree violently on the worth of a charity that helps feed people in Country A, while we might be in total agreement on the worth of a charity that helps feed people in Country B.

The initial subjective judgment that must be made by a potential contributor is whether the risk is great enough to justify the time and trouble that must be devoted to a meaningful evaluation of a charity. When dealing with charities that have been around for years, we can be fairly certain that more than a minimal portion of our donations will go where we intend. It is not much of an assurance. And by donating to only entrenched organizations, we are doing charity itself a disservice. But this approach is certainly far more advisable than decreasing our generosity or turning away from charity altogether. The only other alternative is to invest some time in selecting charitable organizations that will make the best possible use of our money.

The first step is to ask for information. I do not suggest

that you conduct a massive investigation of the charity world. There are certain charitable causes that interest you, and you know at least some of the organizations that serve those causes. Simply select the charities you have been supporting in the past or have been contemplating supporting in the future and write each of them a short letter: "I am interested in the work being done by your organization and I would appreciate your sending me as much information as possible about its activities, including a financial statement covering each of the past three years of operation." If you are interested in only one charity, it is a good idea to send a similar request to a second organization that is engaged in similar work (see Appendix). Several considerations should be applied to the replies you receive.

Availability of Information

An immediate problem arises in the case of an organization that replies to your letter without sending you financial information. Whatever the reason for this failure, it places you in the very unpalatable position of either making a blind contribution or not contributing at all. It is an unkind way to treat contributors.

Possible justifications for failure to supply information vary in worth. Many small organizations claim they cannot afford the expense required to supply us with financial data. We certainly want to encourage both the well-being of small charities and the elimination of unnecessary expenditures throughout the charity world. At the same time, supplying meaningful information to contributors should be accorded top priority, regardless of a charity's size or budget. They don't have to send us a large and expensive annual report. A Xerox copy of their IRS information return will do nicely.

Decent-sized charities cannot claim financial justification

for not supplying us with information. In judging the serious-
ness of their dereliction, the type of activity in which the
organization is engaged can be significant. Health charities,
whether or not members of the National Health Council,
customarily publish annual reports with full financial statements included. A charitable organization in this field that
does not send you such a report has deliberately rejected a
contributor-oriented custom and should be judged very
harshly. On the other hand, some charity fields—notably the
voluntary foreign aid area—have shown a traditional dis-
interest in financial disclosure. In these areas, the organization may be less to blame than the practices that have
arisen around it.

Generally, it seems a good idea to write a second letter to
a charity that interests you but that failed to provide you
with sufficient information the first time around. The second
letter should make crystal clear that you are not taking the
matter lightly and that you want either full information or a
better explanation of why it is not available. If the reply to
your second letter seems unsatisfactory, there are several
appropriate alternatives (see chapter 15). Sending in a
contribution is not among them.

The Annual Report

The standard annual report issued by a charitable organization has several parts, each of interest to a potential
contributor. There is a list of the board members and officers,
usually inside the front cover but sometimes at the end of
the report. The body of the report is devoted to a discussion of what the organization has done during the past
year and what it plans to do in the future. Finally, there is a
financial statement on the past year's operations.

You can gain the most information from an annual report
if you keep in mind certain important realities: First, the

document before you was not thrown together overnight. The people in control of the organization made careful and deliberate decisions regarding the type of paper used, the color of the print, the number of photographs, and the nature of the text. Second, the people who wrote the material are experts in communications, quite capable of conveying facts and ideas in an understandable fashion. The words in the report mean what they seem to mean. If they are vague or confusing, it is reasonable to assume that it was done deliberately. Finally, the report was conceived and executed with the knowledge that it would be read by contributors. Adding these considerations together, it becomes apparent that an organization's annual report can offer us some revealing glimpses of the people who control the charity, particularly as to how they approach contributors and as to what they consider their priorities and responsibilities.

Imagine yourself as the charity executive who designed the annual report now before you. What was your primary objective? Were you out to "sell" the organization, or to report on its activities? To accomplish the former, you would have used a lot of slogans, heart-rending photographs, and such, rather than straight factual material. You would have opted for flowery language, even where it was totally unenlightening and perhaps even confusing. How much money were you willing to invest in items that provided no meaningful information about your organization? Would your annual report have been just as informative on a cheaper grade paper or with fewer photographs of hungry or crippled children?

In making these determinations, we must be careful to guard against our own righteousness. The practicalities of the charity business force even the most publicly oriented charity to devote some of its annual report to selling itself. We should therefore study several annual reports before judging one of them. In any event, it is impossible to make a meaningful evaluation without looking more closely at each section of the annual report.

The Officers and Board Members

This should be the most informative section of the report. After all, the most vital information one can obtain about an organization is the identity of the people who control it. But do not condemn an organization that provides you with only minimal information on this particular subject. As matters now stand, the most any charity reveals in this area is a list of names and, in some cases, an indication that a particular board member holds a prestigious position in the business world. Nevertheless the list is worth a look, for several types of determinations are possible.

For one thing, you should make sure that the organization does in fact have a board of directors or similar governing body. If not even a list of names is included in the report, it is reasonable to assume that such a body does not exist, which raises the very real possibility that there is no organization at all behind the report. You should also determine whether the board is large enough to accommodate a reasonable representation of community interests. This is not to say that most charity boards do indeed accommodate all interests. Quite the contrary is true. But a well-intentioned organization will at least have a board that is large enough to allow for such a possible development. There is no ideal number of board members. Here again, it is necessary to compare several reports before reaching a conclusion.

From the information provided, it may be possible to determine whether the governing body is overly representative of a particular social viewpoint. Doctors, lawyers, business executives, and labor leaders are usually identified by profession or affiliation. Perhaps the most we can expect from

today's charities is that they have a balanced representation
of all segments of the social elite. If even this is lacking in a
particular organization, there is good reason to be skeptical.
Finally, most annual reports state where each board member
resides. There should be members from throughout the
nation. As a practical matter, this factor probably has minimal significance for a charity's policy or operation. But it
does indicate whether there is at least an interest in em-
bracing some divergence in thinking.

The Year's Activities

The major portion of an annual report is devoted to relating an organization's programs, past accomplishments, and
future objectives. This section of the report contains several
types of information, varying in worth. Among the most
valuable is information that helps to clarify the organization's
charitable purpose. It is not something we are likely to learn
elsewhere. The name of the organization tells us its general
area of concern. Of course, within that vast area there are
countless problems that must be solved and countless ways
to solve them. We can seek a cure for a disease, pay the
hospital bills of its victims, or tend to the needs of those it
handicaps. That a charity has included the disease in its
name does not reveal any of these hows, whats, or whos. Nor
does the organization's fund-raising literature offer much
help. It is designed to attract money from people who are
interested in all aspects of a problem, even if the charity is
dealing with only one of them. While the annual report does
not offer the most ideal evidence of an organization's charitable purpose, it is the best that is readily available.

The first thing to do is determine which problems the
organization has *not* been addressing. You can be sure that
if the charity has devoted even a minute portion of its resources to a particular worthy purpose, that fact will be made

clear in the report, probably with considerable embellishment. If it is not there, it is not being done. Indeed, you may well find that the report contains a statement of what the charity is not doing and why, either as a defense against expected criticism or in an effort to honestly inform potential contributors. If you are interested in helping solve a problem that is clearly not within the charity's area of concern, you may well wish to look around for another organization that is working in the same general area.

As for the social problems the charity claims to be addressing, there are two obvious questions: first, whether the organization is, in reality, dealing with them, and if so, whether it is dealing with them effectively. In reading through the report's discussion of activities of previous years, you should give little credence to vague or flowery language, and if possible disregard it altogether. If a program is worthwhile and viable, the report will provide you with a vivid description of how it works and with sufficient factual information to demonstrate how well it worked during the previous year. If you cannot visualize that program and understand it, there is no way for you to consider it in your evaluation of the charity you are studying. Once you pinpoint the viable programs, you should ask whether these are sensible ways to attack the particular social maladies with which you are personally concerned. It should be remembered that in most cases the people who control the charity are knowledgeable in their field and experienced in dealing with the challenges they have undertaken. At the same time, there can be honest differences of opinion among experts. Furthermore, an alleged program activity may have been created as a fund-raising cover or as busywork for unessential employees or as a pacifier for a powerful financial supporter. Finally, it is contradictory in the extreme to advocate charity as a personal transaction and then to suggest that contributors should ignore their personal judgments as to what is charitable. The final judgment is as much your property as the money you will donate to the organization you decide to support. Which of its programs are worthy recipients of your money?

The Financial Statement

There is actually several types of statements included in this section of the annual report. The most informative and easiest to understand is the Summary of Financial Activities. This provides a general accounting of income and expenditures during the previous year. It usually looks like this:

United Health of America
Summary of Financial Activities
Year Ended December 31, 19___

Support from the public:

Received directly:
Contributions $500,000
Special events (less $55,000 in expenses) 30,000
Gifts and bequests 300,000
    Total received directly .... $ 830,000

Received indirectly:
Contributed by associated organizations (after
deducting fund-raising costs of $10,000) 35,000
Allocated by federated campaigns (which
incurred related fund-raising costs of $6,000). 56,000
    Total received indirectly 91,000
    Total support from the public 921,000

Fees and grants from government agencies 78,000

Other revenue:
Service fees 32,000
Membership dues (individuals) 110,000
Investment income 28,000
    Total other revenue 170,000
    Total support and revenue 1,169,000

Deduct support and revenue limited by donor 21,000
    Support and revenue available to finance
    current general activities $1,148,000

Expenditures:
Program services:
Research $110,000
Patient services 87,000
Public health education 210,000
Community services 180,000
Professional education 50,000
    Total program services .... $ 637,000

Supporting services:
Management and general 142,000
Fund raising 251,000
    Total supporting services 393,000

Major property acquisitions 30,000
    Total expenditures $1,060,000

**Excess of support and revenue
over related expenses** .... $ 88,000

The first thing the statement reveals is the source of the organization's income during the preceding year. Income included in the "Received directly" category was raised through fund-raising projects conducted solely by the organization and its affiliates, with no assistance from outside groups such as United Way of America. Income obtained through United Way and similar enterprises is included in the

"Received indirectly" category.[1] The sum of these two income categories is what the organization realized from all fund-raising enterprises conducted for its benefit during the preceding year. The cost of raising this amount is shown in two places: under a fund-raising-expenditure category or in parentheses beside a particular income item, the latter being the case when fund-raising expenses are deducted before any money is transmitted to the organization. Our hypothetical United Health of America raised $921,000 from fund-raising enterprises last year, at a cost of about $320,000 ($251,000 in general fund-raising expenditures and the rest in special-event and federated-campaign costs).

The cost of raising money allocated to other revenue categories is not considered a fund-raising-type expenditure. For example, United Health's $32,000 in "Service fees" was derived from its patient-services program, the cost of which is listed as a separate expenditure item. The cost of obtaining the $78,000 in government grants has been allocated among expenditures for the various programs to which the grants are related. If one of the grants was to finance a seminar for physicians, the cost of submitting the grant proposal would have been included in the "Professional education" expenses category.

The manner in which an organization's expenditures were allocated during the previous year's activities does not offer you ideal or ironclad evidence of what will be done with money you may contribute tomorrow. But it is the best evidence available. Most of the expenditure categories are self-explanatory. But you will probably find at least one category that is too vague to comprehend fully. This arises partly from the fact that life's activities—whether by people or

---

[1] A charity dedicated to full disclosure will show fund-raising costs for special events and federated campaigns beside those income items. Some organizations do not bother to reveal these costs and should be judged accordingly.

organizations—do not happen in neat packages. And when we attempt to pigeonhole those activities, we usually find it necessary to create a catchall category to accommodate the leftovers. In the voluntary health field, for example, it is extraordinarily difficult to pinpoint the "community services" programs of many charities. This does not necessarily mean that there is no worthwhile activity going on in that area. The category is simply too broad to be meaningful by name alone. So in order to understand and appreciate such a program, it is necessary to study specific projects and accomplishments, through either descriptions in the annual report or replies to inquiries you make of the organization.

A continuing problem with health-charity financial statements relates to the muddy lines separating fund raising from public health education. In other charity fields, it is obvious that "public information" is merely another name for public relations, which is really one phase of a fund-raising campaign. In those cases, it would be ludicrous to consider public information a valid charitable program unto itself. It must be regarded as a supporting service and its cost allocated either to management or to fund raising. The situation is quite different in the health field, where victims of a particular disease may be suffering most under the burden of public prejudice or their own misimpressions regarding the nature of their ailment and what to do about it. For them, public health education is the most meaningful and effective program a charity can conduct.

On the other hand, there is much to indicate that many health charities use their public-education programs as fund-raising tools and as parking places for excessive fund-raising expenditures. The National Health Council's standard accounting procedures for charities do not guarantee that all expenditures allocated to public health education are strictly non-fund raising in nature. Indeed, the Council takes a broad approach to what is a public-education expenditure, while stating that informational materials should be charged to fund raising only if they are "explicitly *fund raising* in content or use." Otherwise, says the Council, fund raising can become "a very misleading expense category." The difficulty is obvious. By drawing a narrow definition of what is a fund-raising expense, the Council is making public education "a very misleading expense category."

One type of material the Council says should be charged to public education is that which describes "progress made in preventing or alleviating health or welfare problems." I have great difficulty envisioning that kind of information benefiting anything but an organization's fund-raising campaign. In fact, an essential element in every fund-raising campaign by a health charity is the touting of how much the organization has accomplished in solving the problem it has undertaken to eliminate.

The Council's accounting standards state that in order to be charged to fund raising, informational material or activity should have one of two elements: (1) it "includes as an *essential element* an appeal for financial support of a voluntary agency," or (2) it is "part of an organized fund-raising effort." This leaves a lot of room for interpretation by our charity executives as to what is an "essential element" or an "organized fund-raising effort." And there is every reason to assume that it leaves a lot of fund-raising literature and activity in the public-education-expense category.

This is not intended to denigrate the work of the National Health Council. These are difficult lines to draw, and the Council is the only organization that has shown the slightest interest in trying to draw them. It should be commended for trying. At the same time, we must not lose sight of the possibility that a lot of fund raising may be mixed in with an organization's public education.

You should also keep in mind another fact of life. Just because a charity has devoted some of its resources to a particular project, there is no assurance that the project was well conceived or successful. The amount of money spent in a given area doesn't give the whole picture. The statement alone does not reveal the charity's efficiency, effectiveness, and accomplishments within the program areas it has been addressing. Nor can we be absolutely certain that estimates of employee time were made with accuracy and honesty.

On the other hand, the financial statement is not a flight of fancy. The auditing firm that prepared the statement is undoubtedly reputable and anxious to protect its reputation. The chances of that firm being careless or dishonest in allocating income and expenditures among the various categories are very slim. Moreover, while the auditing firm is usually forced to rely on an employee's own estimate of how his time was spent, chances are good that gross misrepresentations in this regard would be discovered by the auditors. So there are limits.

Just by reaching through the fund-raising literature to a financial statement, you have greatly reduced your chances of being exploited. The possibility still exists—in overly broad and often misleading expenditure categories, in minor misrepresentations that can become significant for the entire organization. You should keep all this in mind and remain wary. But it is certainly better to rely on a financial statement than on the sound of a heartbeat.

The Ultimate Question

In evaluating a charity, you should have only one concern: Does the organization allocate enough of its resources to the cause you are concerned about? Which programs are worthwhile is a matter for your subjective determination, based upon your reading of the annual report and the results of

any further inquiry you may have conducted. Now read
through the summary of financial activities, add up the
previous year's expenditures on programs you wish to support, and compare this amount to the organization's total
support and revenue for that year. This will give you a general idea of how much of your contribution will be spent on
your favorite programs.

In the case of United Health, the organization raised about
a million dollars last year and spent $637,000 of it on
program services. This means that nearly sixty-four cents
of every dollar raised went for the charity's programs, the
rest for supporting services. If a careful reading of the annual report had convinced you that all of United Health's
programs deserved your support, you would now be asking
whether you are satisfied with the organization allocating
64 per cent of your contribution to those programs. If so,
there is no reason to inquire further. It makes no difference
whether the rest of your money will be spent on fund raising,
management, or something else. The only important con-
sideration is whether the charity will deliver enough to the
people or cause you want to help.

If you are not completely satisfied, your next step depends
on whether the allocation of resources to worthwhile programs is, in your view, grossly inadequate or just a little
less than you would prefer. In the second situation, a little
benefit of the doubt would seem to be in order if you have
found the organization satisfactory in other respects: its
board of directors, its willingness to disclose information,
etc. This is particularly true where there is no other charity
in existence that serves the cause in which you are interested.

If the amount being spent on worthwhile programs seems
grossly inadequate to you, there are two alternatives: find
another charity or conduct a further inquiry into the one
you are examining. Should you choose the second course,

the primary thing to consider is where the money that is not getting to your favorite programs is, in fact, going.

In light of the propensity of our charities to sweep excess fund-raising costs under other expenditure categories, the financial statement will probably not show fund raising as the primary short circuit. If it does, and if the organization is well established and espousing a fairly attractive charitable cause, high fund-raising expenditures certainly indicate mismanagement. I do not suggest that you hold fund-raising percentages under a magnifying glass. But when fund raising starts climbing over 30 per cent of receipts, you have reason to believe that the charity is poorly run. You should seriously consider looking elsewhere.

Similar considerations apply to management costs and programs that you suspect of being nothing more than fund-raising covers or busywork for unessential employees. Comparing the financial statements of all health charities, we find that the total of fund-raising, management, public-education, and community-services expenditures rarely exceed 40 per cent of an organization's total support and revenue. For charities in other fields, the total of fund-raising, management, and public-relations or publicity expenditures is usually less than a third of total receipts. This is not to be taken as an ironclad rule, and exceptions must be made for an organization that does have and should have a viable public-education or community-services program. But when supporting services and unidentifiable program costs exceed these figures, there is reason to believe that the organization is mismanaged.

The organization may have overgrown its charitable purpose, leaving a good part of its revenue lying idle, contributions that could be helping needy people being served by other charities. On the organization's summary of financial activities, check the "excess support and revenue" figure for the past three years and compare it to that of other organizations in the field that have similar incomes. If it is significantly higher, too much of what you contribute will help no one.

The organization may have acquired too many employees, becoming too lazy or too careless in supervising them. The annual report should contain a second financial statement: the analysis of functional expenditures. This provides a breakdown of costs within each expenditure category: the amount of salaries, postage, and such that was spent on each program or supporting service. The cost of salaries is the most significant. Compare this item to salary figures for similar organizations—not only the total amount, but also the amount for each program area. Has the organization been spending more for salaries than have other charities? Has it been spending unreasonably high amounts for programs such as research and patient services, usually supported by grants and direct monetary payments? If you have doubts in these respects, do not hesitate to contact the organization.

You will have to make some hard judgments. Do you believe them or not? Do the programs exist or not? Do they really need so many employees? Is the fund-raising percentage reasonable? Here again, much will depend on impressions you build up along the way, founded on the frankness of the charity's replies to your inquiries and upon your earlier reading of the annual report. In the end, you will return to the original question of whether the organization can be expected to devote a reasonable portion of your contribution to worthwhile programs. Before reaching a final conclusion, you should consider one other matter: Does the charity attract and make effective use of a significant number of volunteers, particularly in program areas? If so, it is conducting a separate charitable program that is not reflected in its financial statements. It is providing a way for people to help each other. And many of the people serving as volunteers are retired persons who are seeking ways to lead fruitful lives. While an effective volunteer program should not qualify a totally mismanaged charity for our support, it is a significant factor in deciding whether to contribute to an organization that is not quite what it should be.

I have selected at random four annual reports from my files. I obtained them by writing to each organization, expressing an interest in its work, and requesting as much information as possible on its activities, including financial statements for each of the past three years. I would analyze each of the reports in the following manner:

1 *Recording for the Blind* (*1971–1972*). The report is only twelve pages, and I get an immediate general feeling that the organization is trying to give me a complete picture of itself at the lowest possible cost. The text is succinct. The photographs are informative. There is no heart-tug language. The first few pages set out the charity's sole purpose: providing recorded books to blind students for education, rather than entertainment, purposes. All blind college students and half of our blind high school students have been receiving their textbooks on tape from the organization, upon request and without charge. To me, this seems to be a most impressive charitable purpose. Turning to the financial statement, I learn that the organization received about $1.6 million in 1972 and spent nearly $1.1 million to produce and send out its recorded textbooks, the rest on administration and fund raising. This means that about two thirds of my contribution would be spent on program services. I would like it to be more, but I am satisfied. Moreover, my strong impression from reading through the report is that Recording for the Blind is making every effort to conduct its operations as economically as possible. I would contribute.

2 *United States Committee for Refugees* (*1969*). This is one of several reports sent to me by the organization. Despite my specific request, I received no financial information whatsoever. The report is a collection of essays and statistics on refugee problems. It begins: "The U. S. Committee for Refugees, a Private Citizens Committee, brings the story of the world's refugees to the American people and their leadership in Congress. It encourages support for more than 60 American voluntary agencies working for refugees all over the world and makes funds available to their projects for refugee assistance overseas." I am very dubious. The voluntary relief agencies for which the Committee claims to be encouraging support spend millions and millions of dollars annually on their own promotion. I find it difficult to believe that they need a separate charity to tout them. I am ready to abandon my inquiry. But I notice that George Meany is vice-president of this organization and that its board of directors reads like Who's Who: Marian Anderson, Celeste Holm, Huntington Hartford. I'll put the report aside and make some further inquiries.[2]

3 *Muscular Dystrophy Associations of America* (*1971*). I am immediately impressed with the fact that this organization puts out a cheaply produced annual report, containing only a few photographs and no flowery language. Only three programs are described: research, patient services, and community services. The last is included in the patient-services report and is rather vaguely described. On the whole, the purpose seems worthwhile. Checking the financial statement, I learn that the organization received about $12

[2] They revealed that the organization raised about $130,000 in 1971 and spent 64 per cent of it on fund raising and nearly all the remainder on general administration. The amount expended for assistance to refugees that year was a whopping $3,000. No wonder it failed to provide me with a financial statement.

million in 1971, of which nearly 62 per cent was spent on the two programs that seem most worthwhile to me: patient services and research. I can also see the value of "professional health education," or providing information to medical people, which received about 3 percent of 1971 expenditures. All in all, it seems like a good value. There are some things I wish were different. Public health-education expenses ran nearly $1 million in 1971, half going for salaries alone, with less than $75,000 being spent on printed materials and visual aids. Which indicates two things to me: that part of those expenses were really fund-raising costs and that the organization probably has a bigger staff than it needs. But here again, we're dealing with common practices and it would be terribly unkind to penalize an otherwise decent charity.

4 *The National Foundation* (*1971*). This report is a lavish one—big and beautiful with many photographs. I am not pleased, but I know it is a common practice. I am annoyed at the outset by the fact that the entire report is devoted to only one program: research. It gives me very little to go on in making an evaluation. After nearly twenty long pages of discussion of research projects on birth defects, I am ready to assume that this program is worthwhile. Turning to the financial statement, however, I discover that the organization raised $26.6 million in 1971, only $4.1 million of which went for research grants. This means that less than sixteen cents of every dollar I donate will go to this program. Fund-raising, management, public-education, and community-services expenditures total over $15 million— more than 55 per cent of that year's receipts. There were over $5 million in patient services, but I have no way of knowing to whom they were rendered. Reading through the 1970 annual report, it seems that the organization's patient population is composed almost entirely of handicapped chil-

dren. I know there are several other health charities that
serve the same people and devote more of their budgets to
program services. Rather than reach for my checkbook, I
would probably request annual reports from these organizations.

The method of evaluation I have described should work
well to reduce the risk of squandering your contribution on
wasteful or misdirected charities. It really does not require
much time—perhaps an hour per charity—and it is the
easiest way to obtain relief from that nagging feeling of
being abused as a contributor. I recommend it highly for
all average contributors.

A word of caution: If you are planning to contribute a
substantial amount of money to a charitable organization,
perhaps in the form of a bequest, you should conduct a more
extensive inquiry. Consider several organizations in the field.
Arrange a personal interview with a high executive in each
organization you are considering. Ask for the opinions of
your lawyer and your accountants. It is not enough that
your large contribution will be restricted to research or some
other program. If the organization is mismanaging its
funds and exploiting its small contributors, you are doing the
cause of charity a terrible disservice by supporting any program conducted by such an organization. Be very careful.
The same goes for all of us, of course. There is so much that
is wrong, and we can only reduce the risks, not eliminate
them. We must all be very careful.

15 Contributor Action

Until now we have dealt exclusively with the charity system as it exists—first, by trying to determine how it works, and, during the preceding two chapters, by seeking ways both to protect ourselves against charity promoters and to select the best from among our less-than-ideal charitable organizations. From our viewpoint, these matters have top priority. We know that American charity will not change overnight. In order to put our contributions to good use, we must understand the system and learn how to function effectively within it.

At the same time, it has become more than a little obvious that the system must change. Tomorrow, thousands of our fellow contributors will become victims, simply because they are good people and they do not know what we know about all the atrocities committed in the name of charity. It is an intolerable situation. And its roots seem to lie in two factors: the naïveté of the American contributor and the extraordinary license that has been seized by the people who run our charitable organizations. They have cut us out of the system. They have held us off with glossy photographs and distorted financial statements, while sweeping reality under their thick carpets. Many of them are sincere, dedicated people whose actions are undoubtedly nobly inspired. But it is much too late to examine motives or seek justifications. They have done an appalling job of monitoring our charity system in the public interest. And there is no reason to expect them suddenly to acquire new concern for our interests.

Who, then, should monitor the charity system? Certainly not some government agency that would view our charities through whatever political philosophy happens to be in vogue. Until now, no private foundation or citizens group has effectively met the challenge. This seems to put the burden squarely on our shoulders. Perhaps that is where it belongs. After all, if anyone owns American charity, its contributors certainly do. Furthermore, we cannot deny all responsibility for what has occurred. We have been falling for the myths and slogans. We have been sitting back in our living rooms, salivating to meaningless imagery and celebrity endorsements. Is it any wonder that our charity executives continue to treat us like gullible imbeciles?

Among the various reforms we can support, the least complicated and most realizable is probably a federal disclosure law. Such a statute would simply require any charitable organization soliciting funds through interstate commerce to reveal to each person solicited a financial report on its past year's operations. The law would set forth uniform reporting procedures for the charities it affects, so that we would not have to worry over whether one organization's "fund raising" is another's "public education." Criminal penalties would be provided for willfully misleading contributors or otherwise failing to comply with disclosure requirements. New organizations conducting solicitations would be required to reveal the names and addresses of their officers and board members and to disclose the identity of all fund raisers involved in the solicitation and their fees.

This is not a new idea. I mentioned it to several charity executives and all of them had heard it discussed previously. The only objection to such legislation that they offered me is that people will be confused by the financial statements. They won't understand why charities spend so much for fund raising and such. They may well become less generous with their contributions and our charities will suffer as a result. This fear is probably well founded. But the answer is not to keep contributors in ignorance. Rather, our charities should devote some of their extensive public-relations campaigns to explanations as well as inducements. They should open a meaningful dialogue with the American public. If they tried words on us, rather than the sound of a heartbeat, they might discover that we are intelligent and understanding people, that it is in their best interests to deal with us openly and honestly.

This is the idea behind a disclosure law—not only to provide contributors with information, but also to make meaningful public reaction a major factor in the conduct of the charity business, to induce our charity executives to get their houses in order lest the public deny its support to a mismanaged charity. But the odds are against such a law even being proposed unless people like us take the initiative. The way to do it is through your Congressional representative— by writing letters in which you point out all the outrages of the charity world and ask why your legislator has not proposed legislation to remedy the situation. Suggest a disclosure law and seek a commitment to propose and support such a law. Make a pest of yourself. The only people who can get a law passed are pests and powerful lobbyists. And during the past few years, public-oriented pests have been having an increasingly beneficial impact on our governments.

It will take time, of course; not only for the legislation to be proposed and passed, but also for the executives to respond and the contributors to learn how the system works. We do not have to wait. In fact, there is a very good reason for us not to wait. If and when a disclosure law becomes reality, a lot of charitable organizations in existence today will face a very real threat of complete annihilation by an outraged public. Many of these groups should indeed be discarded. But there are others dedicated to serving truly needy people, people who are not represented by any other charity. If those organizations disappear, it may take years to establish other charities in their place. In the meantime, there will be no way for us to help the victims they are supposed to be serving. For the solution, we must again turn to ourselves.

If you determine, after careful evaluation, that a charity in which you once had an interest is not worthy of your support, take a moment to consider whether there is a public need for a good charity in its place. If so, ask whether you are willing to devote some effort to improving the existing organization. You may be able to work some profound changes without investing an extraordinary amount of time and effort. By spending so many millions on public relations and by being less than candid about their operations, our charities have shown us their greatest vulnerability: fear of adverse public reaction. Couple this with the fact that nearly every reputable charity has its share of executives and board members who are dedicated and sincere—though perhaps naïve or misguided or busy elsewhere—and it becomes obvious that you have an arsenal of very effective weapons.

Suppose you are considering a large health charity that has been in existence for decades. Your major concern is over the organization's enormous public-education and community-service budgets, most of which are composed of salaries. You believe there is an honest need for the organization but that it has grown much too large for its own good and that its employees spend a good part of their time on needless projects. Your efforts to reform the charity might well include the following:

1. A letter to the organization's national office in which you point out your concerns and request an explanation. You receive a lengthy reply which vaguely describes the organization's accomplishments in these areas.

2. A visit to the charity's local office to discuss its public-education and community-services activities. The people are friendly, but they are terribly vague in answering your more pointed questions. You ask for copies of public-education literature. Most of the pamphlets you are given are needless repetitions of other pamphlets. You note that several people in the office have been engaged in lengthy thumb twiddling.

3. A second letter to the national office, in which you request information on the number of people employed in public-education and community-services work, their salaries, how their time is estimated, and so forth. The letter you receive in reply will undoubtedly give some reason for refusing to supply you with such information.

4. A telephone call to a board member in your area (check the annual report, then the telephone directory), in which you reveal what you have been up to, what you have discovered, why you'll never give another dime unless some changes are made. The board member's reaction is not predictable.

5. A letter to the editor of your local newspaper, in which you carefully set out your objections to the charity and relate the nature of your inquiries and the replies you have been receiving. Chances are good that a representative of the charity will send in a reply that will be published. It is now time to encourage your friends to become involved by sending in letters to the editor, writing to the charity, and calling board members. By now you should have developed some specific demands with which the organization must comply in order to improve itself. In this case, you would be wise enough not to ask for a reduction in the public-education budget, but for a reduction in total staff and reallocation of leftover salary money to research and patient-services grants.

In conducting this type of campaign, you may well discover along the way that you were wrong in your initial judgment. If this happens, you should not hesitate to write a different type of letter to the editor, letting readers know that you have discovered a worthwhile charity. It is equally possible that your repeated inquiries will reveal that the organization's problem is a spendthrift executive who has been given too much authority or a board of directors that is too heavily slanted toward a particular interest. Such ailments are very easy to cure, and your efforts may well reap dramatic and immediate reform.

A similar type of contributor action can be used to deal effectively with charity promoters while we await a federal disclosure law. The next time you receive a direct-mail solicitation that seems to come from a charity promoter, write two letters—one to your local prosecuting attorney, enclosing the solicitation letter and pointing out why you believe it is suspect; a second letter in the self-addressed envelope intended for your check, advising the people conducting the solicitation that their solicitation letter is now in the last place they want it to be. They may have broken no laws, but that is up to the prosecutor to decide.

Another method of attacking charity promoters is through mailing lists. From now on, use a different method of spelling your name for each magazine subscription, credit card, and organizational membership. True contributor activists might even want to go back and change their present listings. Keep a record. When the next charity promotion comes your way, you will know who sold your name to so dubious an operation. Write to the purveyor and perhaps to your newspaper. Interesting things may happen. A word of caution: local governments are in the name-selling business. Make sure that the promoter did not obtain your name and address from your auto registration or tax form before assuming that your favorite magazine is to blame.

There is much to be done. Those charity monsters must be chopped down to proper size—their staffs reduced, their piles of redundant literature eliminated, and their programs refashioned in accordance with actual public need. Pretty stationery, fancy offices, executive sports cars, fat expense accounts, high salaries, and all those other non-essentials must be forever banished from American charity. The power grabbing, status seeking and empire building must cease. And those who willfully prey upon the needy and the benevolent must be dealt with harshly and effectively.

We cannot, of course, do it alone. We need the help of

energetic prosecuting attorneys; of concerned legislators; of publicly oriented charity executives and board members; of other contributors who feel as we do, who are tired of being abused and are ready to do something about it. We need new laws to aid our prosecutors in dealing effectively with the charity frauds. We need more reliable and more uniform accounting procedures for charities.

We need all these things and more. But they will not come to us from waiting. And when they come, they will not be put to the best possible use unless some progress has already been made toward breaking down the walls and connecting our charities to their contributors. How will we be able to distinguish appearance from reality, true reform from new public-relations techniques, unless some of our fellow contributors can speak to us from within and assure us that a particular organization has indeed changed? How will our charity executives come to realize that we can all work together with the truth for the sake of charity, unless one organization takes the initiative and leads the way? How can our Congressional representative get that disclosure law off the ground, unless public opinion rallies behind it? What are the chances of such a law working well, unless the present inhabitants of the charity world learn that the road of the future must be a public thoroughfare?

These are the questions for today. These are the immediate challenges. Our old enemies are still out there—self-interest, uncompassion, disdain for truly meaningful charity. They have abused us too long. Who are the crusaders among us? Your time is now.

Appendix:
Finding a Charity

1. *General Listings*. Check the Yellow Pages under "Social Service Organizations" to determine whether there is a group in your area dedicated to the cause in which you are interested. Since some organizations do not appear here, also check the alphabetical directory under "American," "National," the name of your city, or the name of the cause itself. A charity working in a related field may be able to help you. People at your church or synagogue will be aware of certain types of welfare agencies. The Agency for International Development, Voluntary Agencies Division, Wash-

ington, D.C., will send you a list of foreign-aid charities on request.

2. *Health Charities.* Listed below are some charities in this field you may want to evaluate for purposes of contributing. The list is incomplete, and inclusion in the list is not to be regarded as an endorsement. Income and expense figures are taken from reports of the years 1971 to 1973. Since these figures change dramatically from year to year, they are to be regarded only as general indications of how your contribution will be allocated. Only some program items are mentioned. Further investigation should be conducted before contributing.

American Cancer Society, 219 East 42nd Street, New York, New York 10017. Annual income: 79 million plus. Research: 22 million. Patient services: $8.9 million.

American Foundation for the Blind, 15 West 16th Street, New York, New York 10011. Annual income: $5.5 million. Research: $253,000. Recorded reading matter: $1.4 million. Services to blind people: $1 million (this includes cost of appliances that are *sold* to blind people and should be questioned).

American Heart Association, 44 East 23rd Street, New York, New York 10010. Annual income: $45 million plus. Research: $15.7 million. Professional health education: $6.8 million. Community services: $6.5 million (includes nearly $1 million in grants).

American Social Hygiene Association, 1740 Broadway, New York, New York 10019. Venereal disease. Annual income: $600,000. Community services: $200,000. Research: $175,000.

The Arthritis Foundation, 1212 Avenue of the Americas, New York, New York 10036. Annual income: $2.6 million. Research: $1.2 million. Professional education: $320,000.

Damon Runyon-Walter Winchell Cancer Fund, 33 West 56th Street, New York, New York 10019. See chapter 9.

Epilepsy Foundation of America, 1828 L Street, N.W., Washington, D.C. 20036. See chapter 10. Before contributing, present management structure and personnel should be evaluated.

Leukemia Society of America, 211 East 43rd Street, New York, New York 10017. Annual income: $4.9. Research: $1 million.

Muscular Dystrophy Associations of America, 810 Seventh Avenue, New York, New York 10019. Annual income: $13.6 million. Research: $3.3 million. Patient services: $3.6 million.

National Association for Mental Health, 1800 North Kent Street, Arlington, Virginia 22209. Annual income: $1.2 million. Research: $65,000. Public health education: $300,000 plus (such a program seems reasonable in light of the cause). Professional education: $231,000.

National Cystic Fibrosis Research Foundation, 3379 Peachtree Road, Atlanta, Georgia 30326. Children's lung diseases. Annual income: $2.6 million. Research, care, clinics: $1.3 million.

National Easter Seal Society, 2023 West Ogden Avenue, Chicago, Illinois 60612. Crippled children and adults. Annual income: $47.9 million. Services provided directly to handicapped: $29.3 million.

National Foundation, Box 2000, White Plains, New York 10602. Birth defects. Annual income: $36 million. Fund raising: $6.8 million. Patient services: $5.6 million. Public education: $4.5 million. The last item seems rather high and you should determine whether it is a valid and effective program.

National Hemophilia Foundation, 25 West 39th Street, New York, New York 10018. Annual income: $3.6 million. Patient services: $2.4 million.

National Kidney Foundation, 116 East 27th Street, New York, New York 10016. Annual income: $3.5 million. Research: $791,000. Public education: $594,000. Patient services: $470,000.

National Multiple Sclerosis Society, 257 Park Avenue South, New York, New York 10010. Annual income: $12.7 million. Patient services: $1.9 million. Research: $1.5 million.

Recording for the Blind, 215 East 58th Street, New York, New York 10022. Annual income: $1.6 million. Recorded textbooks for blind students: $1 million.

3. *Foreign-Aid Charities.* The following list of charities engaged in this field is, again, only partial. Inclusion in the list

is not to be considered an endorsement. Figures for income and non-program expenditures are taken from reports of the years 1971 to 1973. Here again, such figures can change dramatically, so further investigation should be conducted before contributing.

American Bureau for Medical Aid to China, 1790 Broadway, New York, New York 10019. Medical training, personnel, and supplies to Taiwan. Annual income: $312,000. Non-program expense: $61,000.

American Foundation for Overseas Blind, 22 West 17th Street, New York, New York 10011. Assistance to the blind throughout the world via training, education. Annual income: $582,000. Non-program expense: $214,000.

American Jewish Joint Distribution Committee, 60 East 42nd Street, New York, New York 10017. Supplies and services to Jews throughout the world. Annual income: $25 million. Non-program expense: $2 million.

CARE, 660 First Avenue, New York, New York 10016. See chapter 11.

Catholic Relief Services, 350 Fifth Avenue, New York, New York 10001. Commodities shipped throughout the world. Annual income: $12 million in private contributions, about $100 million in PL 480 commodities and donated supplies. Non-program expense: $556,000. Does not publish meaningful financial statement.

Christian Children's Fund, P. O. Box 26511, Richmond, Virginia 23261. Annual income: $20.8 million. Overseas program: $15.2 million. Supporting costs: $3.9 million. This is the largest of the adoption-type charities which raise funds by soliciting sponsorships of overseas children. Several matters should be carefully considered. Included in "program" costs are such expenditures as translating and handling letters between sponsor and child, and photographs of children—activities that probably benefit the donor more than the recipient and should be considered fund raising or administration. In general, the cost of delivering designated aid is much greater than that of administering self-help and similar projects. Finally, one cannot help but feel that many recipients will be selected more for their physical appearance than need in the sponsorship situation.

Church World Service, 475 Riverside Drive, New York, New York 10027. Commodities shipped throughout the world. Annual income: $7.6 million in contributions, $23 million in PL 480 commodities and donated supplies. Non-program expense: $1.2 million. This organization does not publish a meaningful financial statement.

Foster Parents' Plan, 352 Park Avenue South, New York, New York 10010. See comments on Christian Children's Fund above. Annual income: $11.2 million. Non-program expense: $2.1 million.

Holt Adoption Program, P. O. Box 95, Creswell, Oregon 97426. Arranges actual adoptions, not sponsorships, of needy children overseas; also has several types of community projects in aid of such children. Annual income: $871,000. Non-program cost: $117,400.

International Rescue Committee, 386 Park Avenue South, New York, New York 10016. Assistance to and resettlement of refugees from Eastern Europe, Asia, and elsewhere. Annual income: $1 million in contributions and $2 million in government grants. Non-program expense: $304,000.

Iran Foundation, 350 Fifth Avenue, New York, New York 10001. Health and education projects in Iran. Annual income: $102,000 (this is a 1971 figure and it includes $30,000 taken from reserve funds). Non-program expense: $29,000.

Laubach Literacy, P. O. Box 131, Syracuse, New York 13210. Literacy aids and programs for underdeveloped peoples. Annual income: $642,000 (includes $410,000 in income from various program services). Non-program expense: $121,000.

Lutheran World Relief, 315 Park Avenue South, New York, New York 10016. Commodities and assistance in Asia, Africa, and Latin America. Annual income: $1.7 in contributions and nearly $10 million in PL 480 commodities and donated supplies. Non-program expense: $261,000.

Meals for Millions, 1800 Olympic Boulevard, Santa Monica, California 90406. Food to underdeveloped countries. Annual income: $390,000. Non-program expense: $81,000.

Near East Foundation, 54 East 64th Street, New York, New York 10021. Self-help projects in Asia and Africa. Annual income: $1.3 million. Non-program expense: $121,000.

Pan American Development Foundation, 1725 K Street, N.W., Washington, D.C. 20006. Self-help projects in Latin America. Annual income: $1.1 million. Non-program expense: $228,000.

Save the Children Federation, Boston Post Road, Norwalk, Connecticut 06852. Designated relief and self-help projects for needy children. Annual income: $5.9 million. Non-program expense: $1.1 million.

United HIAS Service, 200 Park Avenue South, New York, New York 10003. Aid to Jewish refugees. Annual income: $2.7 million in contributions and $300,000 in government grants. Non-program expense: $240,000.

4. *General Welfare Organizations.* Some of the most effective groups in this field are local and, of course, cannot be listed. Thus, the following list is more incomplete than those for the other two types of organizations. Again, inclusion on the list does not mean an endorsement. And here again, financial data are always changing. The information is taken from reports of the years 1971 to 1973.

American Friends Service Committee, 160 North 16th Street, Philadelphia, Pennsylvania 19102. Overseas emergency relief, health-care projects, and educational programs; domestic projects for improving our justice system, fighting poverty, drug abuse. Annual income: $7.8 million in contributions and $500,000 in government grants and donated supplies. Non-program expense: $1.8 million.

American National Red Cross, Washington, D.C. 20006. See chapter 7.

Americans for Indian Opportunity, 1820 Jefferson Place, N.W., Washington, D.C. 20036. Education and other assistance for American Indians. Annual income: $250,000. Project costs: $117,000. This is an infant organization, still in development. Reasonable allowance should be made for general administration requirements in early phases of operation. But detailed financial information should be obtained and studied before contributing.

Boys' Athletic League, 51 East 42nd Street, New York, New York 10017. Camps and recreation centers for underprivileged youths in New York area. Annual income: $720,400. Non-program costs: $206,526. Past problems with former employees seem to have been corrected (see chapter 5). But information should be obtained and studied.

Boys' Clubs of America, 771 First Avenue, New York, New York 10017. Operate clubs for needy youths throughout country. Annual income: $1.2 million. Non-program expenditures: $375,000.

Common Cause, 2100 M Street, N.W., Washington, D.C. 20037. Public-interest political action, primarily in Congress and state legislatures. In 1971, its first full year in operation, Common Cause had an income of $4.2 million. Approximately $1 million—27 per cent of total expenditures—was devoted to program activities, most of the remainder to membership recruitment and fund raising. In some states, Common Cause has used membership solicitors paid on a commission basis. It has recorded some commendable accomplishments during its brief existence. However, before contributing, detailed information on financial activities should be requested and inquiries made into solicitation arrangements.

National Urban League, 55 East 52nd Street, New York, New York 10022. Broad range of projects to aid black communities, including job-training programs, health services, family planning. Annual income: $15 million. Non-program costs: $1.1 million.

Planned Parenthood-World Population, 810 Seventh Avenue, New York, New York 10019. A vast conglomerate of domestic and international organizations dedicated to family planning and population control, with a total income in excess of $65 million and operating at around a 10 per cent management and fund-raising cost.

Sierra Club, 1050 Mills Tower, San Francisco, California 94104. A membership organization that engages in several types of environmentalist activity, including legal action on behalf of conservation. Membership fees are not tax deductible as of this writing. But donations to the Sierra Club Foundation can be deducted. The Foundation supports some of the Club's legal activity. Annual income: $3.7 million. This organization does not provide a breakdown of expenditures by programs.

INDEX